A Community of Friends

HAGIOS PRESS

A COMMUNITY OF FRIENDS

THE QUAKERS AT BORDEN

BETTY WARD

HAGIOS PRESS
Box 33024 Cathedral PO
Regina SK   S4T 7X2

Library and Archives Canada Cataloguing in Publication

Ward, Betty, 1923 –
        A community of friends : the Quakers at Borden / Betty
Ward.

ISBN 0-9735567-0-6

    1. Society of Friends – Saskatchewan – Borden –
History – Anecdotes.
I. Title.

FC3549.B67Z7 2004   28936'71242   C2004-905873-8

Printed and bound in Canada

The publishers gratefully acknowledge the assistance of the
Saskatchewan Arts Board and the Canada Council for the Arts
in the production of this book.

CONTENTS

INTRODUCTION

By Donald Ward

MY MOTHER ONCE REMARKED that one lifetime was not enough to do everything she wanted to do. She would have liked to dedicate one life to music, another to literature, another to art, one to family and one to exploring the mysteries of faith. No doubt the list would have expanded as, lifetime after lifetime, the pursuit of excellence opened up yet more possibilities. I was a teenager at the time, and my one life was proving almost more than I could handle; I hope my expressions of appalled disbelief were not as obvious as I remember them. But in retrospect, I can see that she had already made a fair attempt at many of these things. She had been a singer of professional calibre, a sculptor, a journalist, a wife and mother, and a Christian of deep, if eclectic, faith throughout her life. She had the skill, the intelligence, and the grace to pursue any of these goals, whether it might lead her to the stage, the gallery, or the cloister. After reading this manuscript, the distinguished novelist and essayist Sharon Butala spoke of "a hidden story of prairie lives." These lives have been brought to life by a life at least as hidden.

The one thing my mother did not mention in her list of lives destined to be unlived is the thing that stands out most in my mind after fifty-two years of being her son: she has been, all her life, a storyteller. My father was known as a writer and scholar, and had a Leacock Medal and the Order of Canada to prove it, but it was my mother who could weave stories out of the air. When she was finished, of course, they returned to the air — where they remain, for all I know, waiting to be taken up by another storyteller in another lifetime.

This book, then, has a special significance, as it represents a group of stories that were committed to the page before they could escape. Its brevity is deceptive. It represents years of work and research, of painstaking interviews, drawing people out and writing them down. My parents began referring to the "Borden Project" in the early 1970s, and they were still talking about it when my father died in 1990. It was not that my mother couldn't finish it; she just had a conviction that the timing wasn't right. The Quakers would have understood, without question.

Thirty years later — a biblical generation — the timing finally seems to be right. It has been exactly 100 years since Joshua Wake, newly arrived from Birmingham, took up his homestead near Borden, Saskatchewan. He and Hannah have long since been "called home," and many of the young people who populate these pages now have children of their own, and grandchildren. Whether or how much the Society of Friends at Borden has changed since the 1970s is not the concern of this book. It purports only to record how a certain community of people lived out their convictions at a certain time in a certain place. It was written in troubled times, when the world seemed on the brink of nuclear annihilation and humankind was just beginning to grasp the appalling consequences of abusing the environment. But it was written with great love and deep respect, and therefore with hope.

"Neither do men light a candle, and put it under a bushel, but on a candlestick; and it giveth light unto all that are in the house," wrote St. Matthew.

Those who read this book, I trust, will find that the light has extended a little further.

July 2004

TO NORMAN

1. THE FRITCHLEY MEETING

IN 1947 MY HUSBAND AND I had been in the west two years. We had acquired our first child and our first car, and our first trip out of Saskatoon was to the Society of Friends, or Quaker community, at Borden. Word of our coming had gone before us from Friends in Toronto. We were charmed by the names of the people we had been told to contact: Hannah and Joshua Wake. How Biblical, we thought. How fitting.

It was early September, a day of illimitable distance and measureless solitude. There were no fences, no other cars, not another living soul in sight, only fields of grain and stubble, and stands of poplar. The eternal prairie wind was blowing. The landscape was empty, and somehow expectant.

I had enjoyed Saskatoon and the friends we had made there, but I had not been able to come to terms with the landscape. It was in a scale for giants, all those rolling hills undulating to the horizon, the immense bowl of the sky yawning above. I felt terribly exposed and vulnerable. Saskatoon seemed small and isolated, helpless leagues from anywhere. And our first experience of winter had been shocking. We were visiting friends one night when the temperature dipped to -27 degrees F. The cold itself was not the shock; it was our hosts, who insisted that we don some of their warm underthings before walking home. When we demurred, they said, in a manner that chilled me more than the cold, that if we tried to walk across the bridge without being bundled up, we would freeze. Literally.

Norman, being of pacifist views, had been attracted to the Quakers long before we met and married. Anything that interested him, of course, interested me, and we talked about it endlessly. Even so, my first Quaker Meeting in Toronto was something of a disaster. Accustomed in church to the sound of voices raised in song or praise, the minister preaching, I was rather taken aback when the elder of the Meeting said, "We will begin now," and nothing happened. As the minutes ticked by, my anxiety grew. Nobody did anything. Nobody said anything. Nobody moved. Some of them had their eyes shut. Was this prayer, I wondered, or had they all nodded off? I looked at our host and hostess, for we were meeting in a private home, and saw them both contemplating their toes. I looked at Norman, staring into the middle distance, and felt slightly reassured. If he was just sitting there, it must be all right. But what, I asked myself, was going on? Or, more properly, not going on?

I sat through an hour of it, feeling strange and out of place. It was an enormous relief when the hostess finally drew breath and said a few commonplace words, indicating that the Meeting was over. Several people remarked that it had been an especially good one.

Had it? I thought, rather wildly. What had been good about it? Nothing had happened, that I could see. Was I losing my wits?

Apparently not. Quaker Meetings are conducted in silence. Quakers from the beginning have avoided form, on the theory that form is a distraction in itself. So accustomed was I to form in any kind of meeting, especially in church, that the lack of it threw me completely. I still think it odd that, in all our discussions as husband and wife, this had never come up. By the time we contacted the Borden Friends, however, the experience was far behind me, and Norman and I often laughed about it.

Hannah and Joshua had seen us coming for a quarter of a mile, although we had seen no sign of them or the house. Once

A Community of Friends

we left the highway we were entering uncharted seas. There was only a grid road, so called because there was a network of them laid out in grids across the province. They looked perfectly logical on a map, but the prairie was so vast and the long undulations of landscape so slight that individual features blended into it and became invisible.

The Wakes came through a white picket fence in their caragana hedge. Their welcome was low-key, as was their habit, but their smiles were warm and friendly. As we entered their big, low-ceilinged kitchen, the atmosphere was like a benediction, and I felt a comfort and security I had not known since coming to this inhospitable land.

We talked as if we had known each other all our lives. We found we had far more to say than could be encompassed in a single afternoon, so they asked us to stay for supper. I wasn't quite three months pregnant with twins, and the idea of food had been revolting me the whole time. I was thin and half starved. But nothing had ever tasted so good to me as Hannah's fried green tomatoes and her hash-browns with home-made chilli sauce. I could have eaten the lot, all by myself, for it was nourishing more than my body.

After supper we sat talking until the lamps were lit. The wind-charger only worked when the wind blew, and as the wind died down with the evening, so did the electric light. We watched as the last few puffs caused the bulb to flare and dim, flare and dim. When we could see only the filament glowing, Joshua brought out the lamps.

We started for home much later than we had intended, nervous about the road in the dark. But I was feeling a peace of mind and security that had been missing since we first came to the prairies. The distances, the miles upon miles of unfenced fields with no visible signs of humankind except for the growing grain, had truly frightened me. But taking a shortcut across

John Wake's field that night, the prairie didn't seem nearly so forbidding. A handsome coyote leaped onto the track and stopped briefly to stare into our headlights, one paw lifted. He belonged to the night and to the silence and to the track — his track — and by some curious alchemy I felt for the first time that perhaps I, too, could belong in this place and call it home.

All fall, we drove out every Sunday to go to Meeting with our new friends. We would arrive about half past ten in the morning, and there would be little knots of people standing around in the yard of the Meeting House, conversing quietly. When we met Auntie and Uncle, the elders of the Meeting, they were courteous but distant. They were standing outside the Meeting House in the bright autumn sunshine, the wind whistling through the grass at their feet. Uncle snatched at his Quaker hat from time to time; Auntie's bonnet was securely tied under her chin. Uncle's face was stern and sober. We were strangers, and perhaps we smiled too much at a time when everyone was supposed to be "centring down" in preparation for the Meeting. They were both small of stature, but the force of Uncle's personality and the weight of his authority towered above us all.

Years later, we learned that he was a loving father who played games with his children when the work was done. One son-in-law remembered how he always laughed at the old song, "Hallelujah, I'm a Bum," and he liked to listen to "Ma Perkins," a radio program popular in the thirties. He would sit with his ear to the radio and the sound turned low so as not to bother Auntie, and chuckle and chuckle. He offered no word of discouragement when one of his sons joined the rodeo, though others rebuked him for allowing it.

We heard Uncle speak out frequently in Meeting about the "waywardness of the young," reproaching them sternly as "lost lambs." Since no Friend is supposed to speak at Meeting unless

A Community of Friends

prompted by God, I used to think, some of those times, that God was being uncommonly harsh with the young.

When we asked if we could join the Fritchley Meeting, which was what the Borden community of Friends were called, harking back to their roots in England, Joshua was a little surprised. Being a Quaker was a serious matter; he hadn't expected us to move so quickly. He asked that we come back the next Sunday, by which time he would have been able to consult with the elders.

The next Sunday we found Joshua pained and embarrassed. He told us, gently, that it would be better if we did not apply for membership. They were a small group, he said, and they could not afford a split. The younger people would accept us gladly, but the elders could not see their way to it.

"It's nothing you've done," he said. "It's just your bright clothes, Betty, and your lipstick. They don't sit too well with Auntie and Uncle."

My bright clothes? My lipstick?

"Hannah wears a red dress," I pointed out.

"So she does," he agreed, "and Auntie and Uncle don't like it, but they have to accept it because Hannah's a birthright Quaker. They have to accept the fact that Hannah feels easy in her mind about wearing a red dress, and they have to trust her guidance in the matter. With you, they don't, and they're also afraid of your influence on the young people."

Regretfully, we did not apply for membership.

In due course, Auntie died and Uncle grieved. He was lonely, of course, but he waited in faith and serenity to be "called home" himself. He was sure it would be soon. He knew God would not want him and Auntie to be separated for long. But weeks went by, then months. Then a year. And Uncle lived on. He was greatly perplexed, and inclined to feel hurt that God would be so inconsiderate of him. He began to wonder if perhaps there was something more he was supposed to do, some task he had left undone, and God would not let him die until he had done it.

He set about discovering what it might be. He did some pretty thorough soul-searching, accompanied by prayer and Bible reading, and sitting in silence, listening. He consulted a few trusted friends. Finally it came to him: he had for several years been speaking at Meeting "out of his own vanity" instead of letting himself be a channel for God to speak through. He wrote a full account, explaining how he had fallen into error and tracing the consequences of it. When the time seemed right, he got up in Meeting and told the community, apologizing especially to the young, and asking their forgiveness.

It was given, freely and generously. Within days he died, at peace with himself, his community, and with God.

Years later, Norman suggested there might be a story here.

There was.

This is it.

It is not meant to be a straightforward history of a prairie community. Rather, it is a collection of memories, impressions, conversations, descriptions, personal observations, and occasional insights into the Quaker way of life as it was lived at one time in one place. Many of the people who inhabit these pages are now dead — they have been "called home," as the Friends put it with their uncomplicated eloquence — but they are all people I have loved, and it is to them that this book is dedicated; to them and to my late husband, Norman, to whom many of these passages were first addressed.

2. Dear Norman

WELL, HERE I AM, TUCKED UP in this vast, creaking bed, all by myself, with a scalding hot water bottle wrapped in a towel near my feet against the pre-dawn chill. You know how cold it can be on the prairie in April.

I was in a fair state of excitement when I left Saskatoon today, embarking on a new experience, alone. I got to the farm almost in spite of myself. I sailed right past the turn-off and was almost in town before I noticed. At the weigh-station I inquired the way to Wakes' farm. Nobody had heard of the Wakes (they've only been here since 1904). They'd never heard of the Penners, either, although they've been farming co-operatively with the Wakes since the early 1950s.

I backtracked and drove down a likely looking road, watching for the big farm on the left which would be my signal to turn right. But I couldn't find it. Nobody had thought to tell me that it was concealed behind a caragana hedge. So I drove until I came upon the long, familiar banked curve in the road that leads to the Lunds'. I realized my mistake and back-tracked again, all the while keeping the way back to the highway firmly fixed in my mind in case I had to throw in the towel and come home.

When I found the ravine, I went on confidently. And on, and on, and on. When the road petered out in a dirt track, I turned around a third time, vaguely remembering a sign I'd passed a while back — something about a spring garden farm. It was Valley Springs Ranch. There was only one other road to go down, so I went down it. Almost immediately the Meeting House hove into view, and of course the quarter-mile drive into Wakes' is just beyond it. I delicately negotiated a huge mud-hole, and there were Joshua and John, waiting to show me the way to John's house.

Norman, this house is exactly right. It's small and square, divided down the middle. The room to the left has a kitchen at one end and a combination dining/living room at the other, with a stove set to one side halfway along. The kitchen end has an electric kettle, a toaster, a coffee-maker, a hot plate, and an electric frying pan. There is a single extension cord running across the field to Wakes' house, and when you plug in one of the appliances, the light bulb dims alarmingly. Juggling these things promises to be interesting.

The living-room end has a table and chairs and a sofa. The stove is pot-bellied and throws a tremendous heat. John point-ed out the box of firewood, and showed me a pile of dead trees behind the house in case I ran out. The axe and saw are kept in the smaller of the two bedrooms. So you may picture me hard at work, chopping wood, living a pure and sinless life.

The smaller bedroom is full of odds and ends. I plan to keep the door shut and use it as a refrigerator. The larger bedroom accommodates nothing more than this noisy double bed on which I have put every blanket I brought, plus the ones John carted over from Wakes'. It suits me fine, and it was generous of John to let me have it. He often needs to escape from the numerous visitors who descend on the Wakes from time to time, and this little house gives him the safety valve he needs.

I moved in and arranged things to my liking, enjoying it more and more as it began to feel agreeably mine. When every-thing was put away, I went across to Wakes'. As always, I felt blessed as I went in. Hannah was anticipating my arrival with afternoon tea. She greeted me warmly, and was her usual quiet, endearing self. She's wearing her hair in a bob now. It shows more white that way, but she was finding long hair difficult because of her arthritis.

Now it is the end of a long day and I must sleep. I feel lost without you, but I look forward to the next few weeks.

I WAS GLAD OF THAT HOT WATER BOTTLE. At five in the morning the place was as cold as a tomb, but the hot water bottle was still warm, so I cozied up to it and slept another couple of hours. I burnt the toast before getting the hang of the toaster. Hannah came in to clouds of smoke, saying that she and Joshua were walking out to the post box for their morning constitutional, and would I care to come along? Since I was busy burning toast, I declined with thanks.

There are cows in the yard, so I am careful where I step. When I came out this morning a calf was licking the side of my car with evident enjoyment. I took a walk back into the pasture. There are many cattle, and under the Wakes' and Penners' care they are unusually tame. I am not afraid of cows, but these ones are exceptionally curious and I couldn't help reflecting that it would take a lot more than three strands of barbed wire to stop them from doing what they wanted to do if they put their minds to it.

It's a good thing I brought a flashlight. Trips from house to house after dark would be hazardous without it, not to mention trips to the bathroom. The latter, a lowly outhouse, lies across my field and then across Wakes' lawn. It's a long way to go in the dark, with all the cows strolling about. I have thought of making other arrangements, but they all seem dangerous or impractical.

The wind blows endlessly across the prairie. It seems cheerful enough when the sun is shining. But when the sky turns leaden, it blows cold and bleak, and somehow threatening. It laments in the chimney and mourns through the crack in the window sash. Late yesterday afternoon there was a sudden blizzard, with tiny maddened snow flakes whirling crazily in all directions. I thought of the early settlers, utterly isolated, listening to that wind, some of them finally running, screaming from their houses because of it. It got dark quickly when it snowed, and even though I know I'm safe, I couldn't help reflecting that this is the kind of house those settlers would have had, only without the electric cord. When I reflected that these are the very sounds they heard and the sights they saw, I could almost feel their fear.

The prairie is beautiful, but it is an impersonal beauty. You sense its latent ruthlessness, the casual violence that might be unleashed without warning, the sudden, unpredictable changes of mood. I don't believe we will ever really tame these plains. We can clear and plough and sow and reap, build fences and roads and cities, and think we are established and safe. But Nature could move back with one well-timed catastrophe, and it would be as if we had never been.

WHAT A DAY! I went to Wakes' at two o'clock this afternoon and Joshua talked until four-thirty. I came back and typed everything up — twelve pages, single-spaced. The man is a mine of stories and information, much of it fascinating, all of it thought-provoking.

Nancy Penner came to visit when I was finished. She's nineteen now, can you believe it? She knows I came here to work, but I can't work all the time, so I put signs in the window, reading "Available" and "Not Available." As soon as the "Available" sign went up, she came along, and while our suppers cooked — hers in her house and mine in mine — we sat on the front steps and talked of art, my work, farm affairs, and horses.

Nancy wanted to know what exactly I was doing here. She thought I was working on a family history of the Wakes and Penners, and couldn't understand why I'd want to do a thing like that. "Except for Uncle Joshua and his family going back to Hereward the Wake and 1066," she said, "I didn't think we were so interesting that you'd want to write a book about us. Old Hereward wasn't that interesting, either. I've seen the family tree. It looks impressive, but I couldn't make head or tail of it."

I told her it was to be the story of the whole community, and indeed, I thought they were a pretty interesting bunch, even "Old Hereward." Nancy cast her eyes to heaven. "A couple of my brothers might think they were interesting enough to write about," she observed, "but I don't see the point. What's so special about being a Quaker? I've been one all my life and it doesn't seem that special to me."

"You're too modest," I told her. "Didn't you know that the Friends group you belong to is the only one that still follows the principles set forth by George Fox in 1648? All the others have deviated in some way. Yours is the only one in the world that goes right back to the original teachings."

"I didn't know that," said Nancy.

"You're unique on the planet, and nobody's ever told you?"

There was a short silence, then she said, "I kind of wish I'd known. I might have paid more attention."

I wonder what else the young may not have been taught. It will be interesting to find out.

Horses still top Nancy's list of priorities. She has a beautiful black mare she calls Cameo because of the single white spot on her forehead. Next to her horse is her painting. She loves to paint, and spends all her spare time at it.

"What spare time?" I asked.

With all she does around the farm, and helping her mother cook and clean for — how many are there now? Margaret and

Marie are away, so that means Alan and David and Ron, then Nancy and the two youngest, Joan and Sylvia: that makes eight, counting Neil and Betty, the parents. I guess she must get up early and stay up late.

Cows are calving all over the farm. They had eight in one day last week, and this morning a two-year-old lost her calf, and will soon, Nancy informed me, be bawling from a swollen bag, with no calf to milk her.

"They shouldn't breed when they're that young," she said, as though it had been the cow's fault. "At two, they're not big enough, and you generally have to pull the calves out. If you're not there, the calf dies before it can get itself born."

Nancy has birthed many calves, and told me she would come and get me the next time one was coming. I said I'd like that very much. After all, I'm here to learn. A bell rang in Penners' front yard then, and she went off to have her supper and I went in to have mine.

Half an hour later she was back, complete with a horse (which she expected me to ride), and her younger sister Joan, who is thirteen. A cow was in labour in the east pasture a mile back, she said, and I'd have to hurry if I wanted to see it born. I grabbed my jacket but declined the horse, and off we went, Joan and I at a fast trot while Nancy rode.

It was a long mile. We loped around clumps of scrub and rotting snow, panted over huge hummocks of grass, through squidgings of mud and swamp. I was glad of my ankle boots. We arrived just as the cow was getting up from having delivered herself of her calf. But something didn't seem right to Nancy. She circled the animal cautiously, and the cow, strong with instincts, kept turning to face her, ready to defend or attack. The only thing that could distract her was her calf, and when it uttered a thin, mewling sound Nancy was finally able to get behind her.

"Oh, my gosh!" she exclaimed. "The afterbirth has come out, and the womb with it."

She wheeled the horse and tore off at a full gallop, calling over her shoulder, "See she doesn't wander off or lie down on the calf!"

"There's not much we could do about it if she did, is there?" asked Joan, ever practical.

We waited and we watched. We talked a bit, but mostly we waited, and it seemed an eternity. The cow groaned continuously, alternately flopping onto the ground in exhaustion and then getting up again to nose her calf, which was male, Charolais, and huge, Joan said, for a newborn. He moved around some, but he didn't get up on his feet as he should have done.

The sun had dropped out of sight and the bitter cold of the long spring twilight was setting in. I put up the hood of my jacket, and a lone duck whistled by, not a foot above our heads. Something was gabbling in a thicket. Joan said it was a prairie-chicken settling down for the night. Aside from that, the silence was primeval as this drama of life and birth, and quite possibly death, played out before us. My teeth began to chatter.

At last we heard a truck. It stopped at the far edge of the swamp, and Nancy and her father came over on foot, Neil carrying a pail of water and disinfectant.

"Oh, what a hell of a mess," he said quietly. It was the first time I'd heard a Quaker swear. To Joan, he said, "Run as fast as you can. Get Alan and tell him to bring a rifle and the butchering knife. We'll try to save her, but I don't think we can."

The trick was to free the afterbirth. It has tiny, fragile tendrils with little suction cups at the ends attaching it to the womb, and you have to disengage them carefully, one at a time. If they tear, the cow could bleed to death. Once that's done, you try to heave the womb back inside where it belongs.

Working carefully in the gathering dusk, Neil freed the afterbirth in about twenty minutes, talking as he went, describing what he was doing, and why. He sluiced disinfectant over the womb, then he and Nancy together lifted the unwieldy, slithery thing and counted: "One, two, three!" and tried to put it back inside the cow. But as hard as they pushed and manoeuvred, the cow — involuntarily, instinctively — contracted its sides to push it out again.

"She's pushing as hard as we are," Neil said, grunting with the effort. "If only she'd lie down." He leaned his weight on her hip, but the cow wouldn't budge.

"If they lie down, you have a chance," he said, "but if you have to lift as well as push, it's twice as hard."

We were all relieved to hear Alan's truck. He stopped beside his father's, taking in the scene. Joan was with him.

"He's going to try to cross the swamp," said Nancy.

Sure enough, he backed up, gunned his engine, and took a run at it. He came across the swamp on sheer momentum. They needed his headlights to see by, for it was almost dark by then. Where we were standing it was quite dark, in fact, but the sky was still bright. Alan and Nancy and their father all went to work on the cow. They had taken off their jackets and rolled up their sleeves. Nancy had wrapped the wet, still-bloody calf in one of the jackets against the cold. They dipped their hands in the disinfectant and sloshed it up their arms, then each of them got a hold on the womb and positioned themselves, counting, "One, two, three!" and pushed with all their might. But as hard as they pushed to replace it, the cow pushed just as hard to reject it. Time after time they repeated the routine, and time after time the cow repeated hers until all of them were exhausted.

David appeared out of the dark carrying a rifle and a butcher knife. It was so cold by this time that my whole body was shuddering. Seeing him like that, I was seized with an awful apprehension, a cold fright. I am not a country girl. Never had I realized it so fully as at that moment.

"I think it would be best if I went back," I heard myself saying, feeling a coward but not caring. "This is no time for you to be saddled with an outsider."

"You can come back with us in the truck," Nancy offered.

"Look, Nancy," I said. "There are six people here, counting me, and a bad situation. If I leave, there'll be one less to worry about."

Nancy is a sensible girl. "All right," she said. "I'll walk you to the trail."

By this time it was so dark I had serious doubts about my ability to find my way through scrub and brush and heaven knew what else. But the sky was still bright over to the west. All I had to do was keep going toward it — if I could see through the trees between me and it, if I could go in a straight line, if I didn't trip on a root and break my neck, or fall into an old buffalo wallow and knock myself out.

To my relief, Joan said, "I'm going back, too. You can come with me."

We tramped along together in the dark. She knew the place like the palm of her hand, but her idea of walking is my idea of going to a fire, so we covered the mile back about as fast as we had going out.

I was glad to see the light in my little house, and to get back into its warmth. I built up the fire, but it was a long time before I stopped shivering.

I was glad, too, that I had turned away when I did, because we had not gone very far when a shot rang out.

"There," said Joan. "They've had to shoot her."

It has been a full day. I shall sleep this night. I may have nightmares, but I shall sleep.

I DIDN'T WAKE UP ONCE, nor did I dream. But I was up and about early, curious to know the outcome of the night's activities. I found Nancy in the barnyard, talking to a calf.

"Is that the calf?" I asked.

Nancy smiled delightedly. "Yes! Remember the cow I was telling you about yesterday, the one that lost her calf?"

I nodded.

"I found her calf and skinned it, then I put the skin over this little fellow so he'd smell familiar, and I took him to the cow and she accepted him. Mind you," she added, "he's an awful big calf, and he's not getting as much milk as he'd like. But it's enough to get by on."

The calf was remarkably tame. His adoptive mother kept calling him to come away from the two-legged creatures, but he paid no attention.

"Is that because he knew people before he knew cows?"

"Yes," said Nancy. "I was the one who wrapped him up and carried him to the truck and then into the house. He's what they call 'imprinted' on me."

"What did you do with him overnight?"

"We just left him in the kitchen."

I was amazed. "Didn't he make an awful mess?"

"Oh, no. Calves have an instinct to stay where they're put right after they're born, so when I put him down and left him, he stayed there."

"Didn't he . . . uh . . . make a mess?"

"Not a thing. He was exactly as I left him last night."

I've noticed that cows with calves all make a peculiar lowing noise when a stranger comes among them. The calves all go to their mothers when they hear this, except our little Charolais. Nancy said that he would forget his attachment to her in a few days. Meanwhile, he seemed to think that Nancy was his mother and I was his aunt, and it was delightful.

"What did you do last night?" I asked, scratching among the soft hair on the creature's neck. "Joan and I heard the shot. . . ."

"Well, first we milked the cow."

"Really? What for?"

"That first milk has special things in it. We couldn't expect him to do well if he had to do without it. So we milked her, and gave him that, and then, well, we came home, like I said."

"What did you do with the cow?"

"We left her."

"You mean she's just out there lying down dead? If I take a walk that way I'd find her?"

"In a few days there'll be hardly a sign she was ever there."

This was all new to me. My face must have registered my conflicting emotions, because Nancy was patient.

"A cow's no good right after she's calved," she explained. "At least, no good as food for people. But the coyotes and foxes need food, too. Whenever we have to do something like that, we leave the carcass for the other creatures, as long as it's not diseased."

I don't know if that was something that should have been obvious even to a city person, but I was surprised that they cared enough for the creatures who shared their land to think of their needs instead of disposing of the cow in a way that was more profitable to themselves. But when I thought about it, it seemed natural, and just.

"How do you skin a calf?" I asked thoughtfully.

She looked at me as if she thought anybody with a grain of common sense would know how to do a thing like that. Then she began, "You take a sharp knife. You circle the ankles and start peeling. . . ."

Rather hastily, for I had not yet had breakfast, I said I didn't think I needed to know anything more about it.

3. Coming West

Wakes' house was long and low and white, banked all around with earth so that it nestled into the landscape as if it had grown there. Surrounded by a thick, high hedge of caragana, you wouldn't have known there was a house there at all except for the low white gate in one corner of the hedge. Through the gate and along a well-worn path to the back of the house, there was one of those outer rooms that every farm house has: a catch-all for muddy boots and jackets and hats and anything else you might not want to take into the house. The Wakes kept their cream separator there, along with a ship's model Joshua had built, and a model train engine.

A door led into the kitchen, a multi-purpose room that was always redolent of Hannah's bread in some stage of preparation. Beyond was the living room, rarely used because it was uninsulated and difficult to heat. But as family members began to retire and had more leisure, they insulated it, acquired some comfortable furniture, and installed a space heater.

Over the years, as they needed more rooms, walls were knocked down and out-buildings attached to the house until there were four bedrooms, side by side, along the back. Two of them opened off the living room, and were occupied by the two unmarried Wake brothers, John and Billie. Billie was hardly ever there. A small guest bedroom shared an entry with the cellar, and the master bedroom, a spacious former granary with beautiful big windows, was behind the kitchen. The kitchen and living room were built from the packing cases in which their belongings had come out from England.

"If you took the wall-board off the ceiling," Joshua told me, pointing, "you'd see Hugh Wake, Saskatoon, North West Territories printed on it. The walls along the west side are partly packing cases, too. We had to use every scrap we could get."

William McCheane (pronounced MacShane) had come out in 1903, a year before the others began arriving. Somebody had to come out and "case the joint." McCheane was accompanied by another William named Kennedy.

Now, Kennedy was a Quaker too, but he was also something of an entrepreneur. He had helped organize the Galicians and the Doukhobors when they came to Canada in 1899, and when he heard that the Quakers near Birmingham were interested in Canada's offer of land, he began corresponding with the Canadian government. There was a large number of them, Kennedy wrote, and they wanted to settle near to each other. The authorities agreed to set aside a tract of land for them, but only "insofar as it is possible for us to do so," for squatters were coming in and they had rights, too.

The land set aside for the Quakers was west of Saskatoon. Sir Clifford Sifton himself assured Kennedy and McCheane that it would be held for them until they arrived the following year. But letters of the time, dated 1903, make it clear that, in the bureaucratic mind at least, "Quaker" was synonymous with "Doukhobor" — one supposes because of their common pacifist views — and the Quaker land was adjacent to that of the Doukhobors. It is also clear that there were squatters on the land. The squatters were told that the land was being held for the Quakers, but they knew about squatter's rights, too: if a person builds a shack and lives in it and works the land, it doesn't matter what anybody says, it's the squatter's land. A good many of them had done just that, to the annoyance of a good many

When William McCheane arrived in 1903, in fact, he .id that the best land had been taken by squatters.

William Kennedy wrote to Ottawa, Winnipeg, Prince Albert. He wrote to Ministers of Immigration, Land Agents, Commissioners of Dominion Lands, Ministers and Deputy Ministers of the Interior. His letters were passed from one official to another; officials wrote to other officials on the matter; third parties wrote, reviewing the situation. This went on for the better part of two years. The correspondence runs the gamut from impatience to irritation to exasperation.

Poor old Kennedy — starting off so hopefully, signing his letters in the flowery style of the time: "Thanking thee for thy promised assistance and past courtesy, I am, thine sincerely," or "Thine obedient servant, William Kennedy." By 1905 he was signing his letters simply, "Very truly." Even Quakers come to the end of their patience.

By the end of 1905 the confusion was total, and the land in question was thrown open for anybody who wanted to file for it. This was hardly fair to the Friends, many of whom already had buildings up and ground broken. William McCheane, in fact, had filed for his land and paid for it in Ottawa when he'd been there with Kennedy in 1903, but the Land Titles office in Prince Albert had not been notified so he had no receipts. The week before Christmas, he had to go to Prince Albert and file for his land and pay for it again, or lose it. He was in his sixties at the time, and you can imagine what travelling was like back then, and at that time of year.

Joshua was philosophical. "The squatters were there, and that was that," he said. "We had no intention of quarrelling with them. We just did the best we could with what there was. McCheanes had picked out their quarter section by the time my father and I got here, and their house — the first in the district — was already half finished. John McCheane and I picked

A Community of Friends

out this one of ours. We didn't know much about such things, but we weren't stupid. We talked to people, we read government pamphlets, and we ended up helping quite a few people pick out their land."

In the government's defence, it must have been a monumental task trying to keep track of such an immense influx of people into such a large and unknown territory. It makes you wonder how anything was accomplished at all. How lucky we are that we're a couple of generations past all that. I don't think I'd have made a very good pioneer.

JOSHUA WAS EIGHTEEN in 1904 when he and his father, Hugh, came to Canada. Hugh was a carpenter by trade, but ran an ironmonger's shop in Birmingham. They were a large family, and he wanted better opportunities for his children than they were likely to get in England. When the Canadian government offered land to anybody who wanted to farm it, he jumped at the chance, even though he wasn't a farmer. Apparently, all sorts of people did that. Passage from Liverpool to Saskatoon cost them $30 each.

The ship was a small one, and pitched dreadfully. Everybody was seasick. The dining-room held about twenty people, and beyond that a narrow passage led down to the cabins. Joshua and Hugh went second class. Second-class cabins contained two uppers and two lower births each, with just enough room to get dressed in between them, and a wash basin at one end.

Behind the dining room wall was the big casing of the engine room, and they could hear the engines going down below while they were eating. Joshua remembered how the engines sounded: NO-I-DON'T . . . NO-I-DON'T . . . NO-I-DON'T . . . NO-I-DON'T. . . . And when the sea was rough, the propellers would come out of the water and it would be NO-I-DON'T-NO-I-DON'T-NO-I-DON'T-NO-I-DON'T.

There was a burial at sea when a crew member died. The water was clear, and it gave the passengers a queer feeling to see the weighted body tipped overboard and sinking down and down. "But the saddest," according to Joshua, "was when a man disappeared a few days before we were due to land. They searched the ship from stem to stern, top to bottom, and decided he must have jumped overboard. It was the saddest sight, his baggage set out, waiting to be taken back to England."

When they were close to Canada it began to snow, and they ran into ice coming out of the G ulf of St Lawrence. The floes got thicker and more numerous, and finally the boat had to stop. The people of Quebec City and Montreal had been hauling their garbage onto the ice all winter, and when the ice went out, so did the garbage. They were ice-bound for two days amid the household detritus of Quebec. Several other ships caught up with them, and eventually they "tailed in," one behind the other as the front ship blazed a trail through the ice, and at night all you could hear were the ships blowing their horns as they tried not to run into each other.

The sea crossing took fourteen days. At Quebec City the ship off-loaded crates of glass from Birmingham and took on squared timbers to go back to England. Then it continued on to Montreal to let off the passengers. The train trip to Regina took another four days. Joshua and Hugh had packed a box of food before leaving Birmingham, as meals weren't provided. They brought tools with them, too — chisels, saws, hammers, planes; the government allowed space for what were called "settler's effects," and they'd heard that carpenters were doing well in Saskatoon.

The first thing Joshua did on landing was buy a thermometer. "And I want it to go down to sixty below zero!" he informed the surprised clerk.

"Where are you going?"

"To Saskatoon,"

"Ah." The clerk's face cleared. "I'm told it gets so cold out there that when you want to blow out your candle, you have to break off the flame. Moreover," he went on, "the summers are so hot you can fry an egg on a rock."

The train left Montreal through the suburbs, passing block after block of back yards full of laundry. It was a Monday, and the Wakes were reassured by the sight. People washed in Canada, just like they did in England!

It was a colonists' train, with slatted wooden seats. "All right for sitting in the park," said Joshua, "but pretty rough to sleep on. Father and I slept sitting up, in blankets. By then it was May, and not too cold."

Joshua thought the scenery was wonderful. "From Hornpayne to Winnipeg there was nothing but rocks and trees and hills. Once we stopped in a town in northern Ontario, and I saw some Indians mending a canoe. I went over to have a look, and sure enough, it was real birch bark."

Their first sight of the prairie surprised them both. Joshua had imagined the flatness, but, "I'd no idea that flat could be that flat!" They arrived in Regina during spring thaw, and there was water everywhere. In the Lumsden valley, five miles of track were under water, and only men were allowed to go on. Women and children were kept behind until the water went down and the tracks were safe.

"We got across the five miles in boats," Joshua remembered, "and then we went another five miles in a wagon, then there was a train. We were lucky, because the bridge was out at Saskatoon and no trains were coming or going, north or south, except for ours."

It was a freight train, and it took three days to cover the 160 miles from Regina to Saskatoon. The track was so bad that the engineer ran the train only in daylight, and then slowly. At night the men slept in box cars, uncomfortable and cold.

When they got to Saskatoon, they crossed the swollen river in a ferry called the Qu'Appelle, and went to Immigration Hall where newcomers could stay free of charge. Joshua and Hugh stayed for two weeks, until their gear arrived from Regina. They'd found no work, and they were down to their last nickel. They bought a loaf of bread with it, and once they had secured their tools they recrossed the river to the east side, then known as Nutana.

Where they landed on the Nutana side was eventually called five corners because of the five streets that converged at the top of the Broadway bridge. But then it was mostly grass, with a few stores, and an implement shed run by a woman named Grace Fletcher. Hugh and Joshua got a month's work putting a new roof on the shed. Then in July 1904 they set out, learning that their friends the McLeans had arrived in Canada and were settling in the district.

Their first house was built of sods. First they put up corner posts, with framing joists on the top to make a rectangle nine feet by sixteen. They cut poplar trees three or four inches in diameter and laid them at an angle against the joists. They cut the sods about fourteen inches wide, sixteen or eighteen inches long and five inches thick, and laid them around the frame, one over another, until they reached the top of the wall. Above the roof line they hoisted one or two ridge poles, and from the edge of the roof to the ridge poles they laid more poplars, until they had a fairly solid frame.

"But you had to keep those poplar poles dry," Joshua explained, "or they'd rot through in a few years. So what we did was cut a lot of thin willow bushes and strewed them around, with loose hay on top, and if we had tar paper we'd put that on top, too. Then we laid the sods over it. We put in windows — not very many — and built inside walls and plastered them to keep out the drafts, and calcimined them. Those houses were warm in the winter and cool in the summer."

A Community of Friends

But they weren't proof against the mosquitoes. It was an unusually high run-off in 1904, which meant an unusually high population of mosquitoes that summer. They had no screens for the windows, so people couldn't sleep at night, and the animals were always distracted. Horses would go mad trying to get away from them. Joshua remembered running his hand along the flanks of a white horse they had that summer, and leaving a red smear of blood from all the mosquitoes on it.

They were just in time, in 1904, to see the last big prairie fire. It swept from Battleford all the way to Borden, and would have gone on indefinitely but for the river. Every settler knew that the first thing to do was make a fire-guard around the buildings and the pasture. It was a simple enough procedure: you ploughed a few furrows well away from the buildings, then you went outside that and ploughed a few more, and burned the area in between.

Even so, one prosperous farmer lost everything he had.

"Didn't he have a fireguard?" people asked.

"Oh yes," was the reply, "but he forgot his road, and the fire came down the grass between the tracks."

You couldn't be too careful.

IT HAS BEEN A WEIRD FEW DAYS ALTOGETHER. You know there is a pattern to some spans of time: if a day starts out with, say, a startlingly fat person crossing your path, you may encounter whole processions of them parading through the rest of it. In an ordered universe, these contradictions of comfortable logic persist.

To set the stage, you will have to picture the surroundings. This house of John's isn't insulated, but it's lined, and the walls are calcimined in light blue. On the outside are shingles, weathered to a silver-grey. The house stands in front of a row of Manitoba maples. Aside from these, it is at the mercy of the elements, which come at it from three directions, and sometimes over the trees and down the chimney from the fourth. This is the only building here that isn't hidden behind caraganas, so to look out my window is to see how the raw prairie must have looked. The lawn is original prairie wool.

I took Thursday afternoon to type up my notes. In my mind I was back in the time of no electric lights, no amenities, unreliable water, few neighbours. Gradually I became aware that I could hardly see, and there was a loud noise outside. The fire in the stove crackled suddenly, and a puff of smoke came out the front as a gust of wind whooshed down the chimney. It startled me.

Then something scratched at the window. I looked around and felt the hair rise on the back of my neck as a huge round thing, all twitching tentacles, scrabbled with ghostly fingers across the window pane. Rooted, I watched it fall away. Then with a tremendous roar of wind it came back. Agitated and trembling, it fell along the window, clawing, entreating, imploring, until finally, with a truly dreadful shrieking of wind the headless, many-fingered apparition fled into the horrid dark.

It was a tumbleweed. But seeing it like that, my mind far in the past, I also saw it the way a civilized Englishwoman might have seen it, alone in her cabin in the middle of nowhere, her husband working miles away. For her, this would have been a spectre of the mind, harking back to unremembered myths and ancient horrors. She would never have seen anything like it in her life.

All night the wind shrieked and howled, yet in the morning all was sweetness and light. Bland innocence. Sun and warmth and gentle breezes. I worked until sunset, put my dinner on to cook — it would take about forty minutes — and went out for my usual walk. I followed an old track that runs along a field, with a bluff of trees on the other side. The Wakes say the track was there when they took over the place, so it must be old indeed. It is quite deep, worn into the ground like a trough. I was delighted when I found it, and have often taken walks on it before dinner or when I needed a breather.

The sun had set, and the long, serene twilight was lovely. But suddenly I felt cold, and there was a prickling in my scalp. Something, or somebody, was there. I could feel it. I looked all around me. Nothing. What nonsense, I thought. But the sense of something watching me grew stronger. It became menacing. Still I walked along, trying to pay no attention. But the feeling reached such a pitch that I could almost hear something screaming, Get out! I became so frightened that I ran all the way back to the house.

This sort of thing makes you curious, so when Nancy and I went for a walk this morning, I nodded toward the old trail. "Is there . . . something . . . down there?" I asked.

"What do you mean? What sort of something?"

I hesitated. "I'm not sure how to phrase it. Last night I was walking along that track and something scared the living daylights out of me. There was nothing there, but I ran all the way home."

After a moment, Nancy said, "So you noticed it, too. Joan and I thought it was just our imaginations."

We walked along in silence. She obviously had something more to say. Finally, she stopped.

"There are some nights," she said solemnly, "that I would not put my foot out the door. There are some nights I wouldn't open the door even a crack. I don't know what's out there, but I know it's bad, and I don't want anything to do with it."

4. The First Years

THE WEST WAS MISREPRESENTED in advertisements overseas. The winters were described as "bracing," while the heat of summer, the hordes of mosquitoes, and the everlasting wind that drove some people out of their minds were never mentioned. Overseas ads also claimed that good, sweet water was plentiful, which may have been true, but many early settlers were hard put to find it. Slough water was drinkable in the spring, but it soon became brackish. Many people dug wells beside sloughs, hoping that the seepage from slough to well would filter the water. Sometimes it worked, but it was still very strong and, if you weren't used to it, extremely laxative. Canny settlers drank tea by the gallon for two reasons: boiling sterilized the water, and tea disguised the awful taste. Threshing gangs had their water hauled from the river.

Those first years were an endurance test for the Friends at Borden. Of those who had means, some returned home. Even the cheerful and optimistic Joshua said that if one thing could have driven him back to England, it was the mosquitoes. Many people ordered netting from catalogues, in the meantime enduring as best they could the billions of insects that bred in those wet years. Beekeepers had hats with netting, and wore them day and night. Everyone built smudge fires of wood laid over with sod and manure. They set up a tremendous smoke, and many people sat by them all through a long, hot night when they couldn't sleep anyway. The beasts suffered quite as much as the people, if not more so, and would rush pell-mell for a newly lit smudge fire, knowing somehow that relief would be found there.

Joshua worked for William McCheane his first years in Canada, with McCheane's sons, John and Edward. They were out haying when some unexpected allies in their constant battle against the mosquitoes appeared. Edward recorded in his diary how "cloudless day followed cloudless day, and at intervals a swarm of small blackbirds would arise, darkening the very sky for a moment. Then a hum of wings, and they would settle all around us, on our hats, the horses' backs, to catch the mosquitoes and flies, and seem to have no fear. They make the place pleasanter and less lonely where human hearts are as yet few and far between."

Edward McCheane wrote about everything he saw, and commented at length on the raw immensity of the land, and how small and alone it made him feel. "It is a very deplorable condition to be in," he wrote after a three-day trek to Saskatoon for supplies, "on a vast prairie of millions and millions of acres where you can't ask the way of a policemen on the corner, in this land of no hedges."

Joshua and Edward had loaded the wagon as full as they could, but walked themselves so as not to make the load any heavier for the horses. After thirteen hours or so they stopped at one of the Doukhobor villages and asked for accommodation for the night. The Doukhobors were always hospitable, and glad to make a little extra money.

"The Doukhobors were very civil though their manners seemed very oriental to us," Edward recorded. "While putting up the horses, a quantity of water ran down my neck and as there was only a fowl roost above, I was a little surprised. Leaving the stable, I saw an old woman watering her cabbages on the roof where she had her garden."

When they went into the house, they asked if they could wash. Language was a problem, though, and when they were each handed a cup of water they drank it. When they handed back the cups, the housewife refilled them. When they drank that, too, the good woman seemed astonished. They tried to explain by gestures that they needed soap and towels, and eventually the women brought them, along with two more cups of water. Realizing they must be encountering a different custom of some sort, they managed as best they could, pouring a little water into each other's hands and washing themselves that way.

A little later, the family washed for supper and Joshua and Edward saw what they were supposed to do. From ancient necessity their hosts had had to conserve water. They each took a mouthful from the cup and drizzled it into their hands, and with that they cleansed both hands and face.

"It is an ingenious way to save water," Edward observed, "but I prefer the old English method."

He commented on the simplicity of the Doukhobor life, but deplored "the ridiculous waste of wood" in their solid log houses. Had he realized the ferocity of the winter ahead of him — his first in the new country — he might not have been so dismissive, for his own home was but "one board thick."

Later he described how he and Joshua had had to bed down: "They have a wide bench all around their room which they convert into beds at night. We had to comply with their customs and sleep with the family."

Joshua, for his part, said he was tired enough to sleep anywhere.

In the morning, they were given an ample breakfast of potatoes and eggs, bread, and tea, "for as you know," Edward wrote, "the Doukhobors are vegetarians. Their homes are scrupulously clean, and they charged us 25 cents for lodging for three horses and two of us, which we thought very reasonable."

When the West was opened to European settlers, many of the ranchers who had first started to trickle in after the railway went through in the mid-1880s had to move on. For the newcomers were farmers who would be growing grain, and the land could not support both lifestyles. When Joshua and his father came to Canada in 1904, there were still many ranchers in the area.

"There was a huge ranch just north and west of here," he told me. "It must have been a good thirty-five, forty thousand acres. It was run by three men: Church, Richardt, and Sherratt. Sherratt was a Métis. He lived on the river bank where Valley Springs Ranch is now, and he was immensely wealthy. A lot of people worked for him those first years.

"Those three men had thousands and thousands of cattle. It took two years to round them all up and trail them to Regina — two months for each lot of a couple of hundred head. It was all open country, and plenty of good prairie wool for them to feed on."

Many people found it a stirring sight to see all those animals on the move, but David and Lydia Crabbe did not. Lydia was Caroline and William McCheane's daughter, and the quarter section she owned with her husband David adjoined her parents'. The cattle trail, which was very wide, ran beside the senior McCheanes' property but directly across the Crabbes'. David and Lydia had done some ploughing but, with hundreds of cattle likely to be driven across it at any time, they were understandably hesitant to build any kind of dwelling. Then they heard about a local man who was saying that, since there was no building on it and it was not reserved land, he was going to squat on it "in spite of McCheane or anybody else." Something had to be done, and quickly. That same night, David and Lydia set up a tent, took a team of oxen, and spent the rest of the night ploughing.

As luck would have it, Sherratt set out at dawn that morning with three hundred head of cattle. David and Lydia were still in bed whey they arrived. Edward left an account of the event in his diary:

> The great herd of cattle stampeded around our home last night and made a raid on David's tent about 5 am. They would soon have had the tent over had not David fortunately got Harry Kennedy's gun there, and as they made five charges David gave them five charges of shot in exchange. They did not appreciate this but making off to a fair distance, made raid after raid on the little tent. David, inside, waited until their heads were close and as one of them lowered his horns to charge past him he fired, shooting him square between the eyes with #4 shot. This was more than he expected . . . and . . . he closed his eyes, turned a backwards summersault landing on his four feet, then made a rush in the opposite direction half mad with pain.

All the others cleared off after him, to the satisfaction of David and Lydia who were stopping day and night on the land until the squatter cleared off.

Throughout the two years it took to move the herd, the McCheane household was regularly subjected to the shouts of the cowboys, the bawling of the cattle, and the dust of their passing. Trouble and nuisance they may have been, but there were benefits. One day a new-born calf got stuck in a thicket and the cowboys had no time to get it out. The McCheanes rescued it, and that single calf was the start of their herd. Another time a filly found herself too exhausted to go on by the time the herd had reached McCheanes'. She, too, stayed, and grew up to foal a number of colts that were renowned in the district for their speed and breeding.

The McCheanes, by virtue of the fact that they had built the first house, had the first post office in the district, which had to have a name if mail was to be delivered there. William McCheane, who knew his legends, called it Halcyonia, for the halcyon days "which are the calmest, most peaceful days of the year, when the kingfisher builds its nest."

The McCheane residence was used as the Meeting House until the community built one in 1915. It was also the place where newcomers stayed until they had picked out their land and erected some sort of shelter. This was hard on the women of the family who did the cooking and the laundry and the washing up. Caroline was in her sixties, but she never complained of the work. She endured the bitter cold of winter without complaint as well, but it was hard on her. The house, while attractive in appearance inside and out, was cold and draughty. The animals in their sod barns were better housed and more comfortable than the family.

One frosty day, a knock came at the door. There was one of their Doukhobor neighbours, pointing out the "steam" — their precious heat — that was escaping from under the eaves of the house. He showed them how to make a plaster of clay, straw, and horse manure to chink the cracks. They were grateful to him.

"We were used to draughty houses in England," Joshua said, "and we'd no idea that drafts in this country could kill you."

Joshua worked for William McCheane for two years, at the going rate of $25 a month plus room and board. (The railway paid $30, so they could keep workers who might otherwise have run off to work with the threshing gangs at harvest time.) The senior McCheanes did no farm work, but ran the post office and kept the house going for the many visitors. The eldest son, John, lived with them, also Edward, and an unmarried sister, Hannah Mary. Joshua, who could handle horses, looked after such things as driving the teams for the binder and other farm implements.

In November 1904, Joshua had his first — and very nearly his last — experience of a prairie blizzard. He and William McCheane had gone into town one morning for supplies. They started for home, the wagon well-loaded, in the afternoon. The cold was biting, and soon it began to snow. Neither man had ever seen snow like it before. It came down like flour from a sifter, thick and fine, and soon filled in the ruts and valleys, obliterating every recognizable landmark. When they ran into the frozen creek, William McCheane asked, "Does thou know where that is, Joshua?"

"Yes, I do," said Joshua, because at that moment he did, though he wasn't so sure about the rest of the way. But he was an intelligent young man, and he knew the creek ran north to south. The house lay to the east of the creek. If he could keep going straight east from where they were, he reasoned, he would eventually feel the wagon wheels hit the ploughed fire-guard, and from there he could follow the furrows to the house.

"The first thing I did was point the horses in the right direction," he said. "Then I noticed the exact angle the wind struck my face. I kept my hat tilted and my collar turned down, to be sure and feel it exactly right all the time, and I started the horses off. I had a terrible job keeping the horses going in the right direction. Like all horses, they wanted to pull around so the wind was behind them. I kept hauling them around and hauling them around, feeling for the angle of the wind, and finally the wagon wheels struck the furrows a quarter of a mile south of the farm. We followed them and got home safe and sound."

In the spring of 1905 Joshua, with John McCheane, broke eighty acres at McCheanes' with horses and oxen, and nineteen acres on Joshua's own farm.

"All my wages went into my farm," Joshua said. "William McCheane didn't pay cash, it all was in kind. I used his implements, and we balanced it out that way."

The following winter Lydia Crabbe came down with typhoid. She and David had moved to the town of Radisson, eight miles from Borden and nineteen from her parents' home, when the railway went through in 1905. She was delirious with fever. At first, David looked after her and the baby, but then he came down with it. Lydia's sister, Hannah Mary, went to look after the three of them, but Lydia had to be watched day and night, and it wasn't long before Hannah Mary got it, too.

There had been a doctor in Radisson, but he left as soon as the typhoid hit. It fell to Joshua to find someone to take care of them all. He went around the district, from house to house and farm to farm, and finally found a registered nurse named Mary Booth, who went to stay with the Crabbes. The baby stayed with another family.

All the time Mary Booth was there, Joshua drove the nineteen miles to Radisson whenever he could, to see how things were, and then came back to McCheanes' to do the chores. Hannah Mary began to recover first. When she was well enough that her mother could take care of her, Joshua covered a wagon, put a stove in it with a straw mattress and blankets, and he and Caroline McCheane went to get Hannah Mary.

"As soon as we got going, I could see that the trip was going to be rough, so I drove the horses hard to get Hannah Mary home as quickly as I could. We never stopped. We went as fast as we could the whole nineteen miles, and got her home and into bed. Even so, she had a relapse, and we thought she'd never pull out of it. But she did.

"I'd run those horses so hard they were wringing wet, and the barn was bitterly cold. I was afraid they'd get a chill and die. But I rubbed them down with dry cloths, and then I strapped horse blankets over them — it's important to keep horses warm and dry — and they came through all right, too. That was the only time in my life I ever did that to horses."

Mary Booth was always cheerful, but the next time Joshua went to see how David and Lydia were getting along, she said she was through. She was played out and done in, and told Joshua that he'd have to get somebody to take over.

"Where on earth was I going to get someone else? It was Christmas, and cold, so cold. But I went around the neighbourhood again, from farm to farm, and about ten or eleven miles away I found a Miss Robinson who said she'd come. I'd got there late, and had to stay overnight. The next day was Christmas, but Miss Robinson said she'd go right away, Christmas or not, and she did."

With typhoid, it took about three weeks for the sufferer to reach the "crisis," then you'd know in a few hours whether the person would recover or die. If they recovered, it took another couple of weeks for them to get back on their feet. It was more than a month before Lydia and David started to get better.

BLIZZARDS AND EPIDEMICS, doctors who moved away when sickness struck, no telephones, no electricity except in the towns: it makes you marvel at the human spirit that any of them survived at all.

Joshua remembered another blizzard that struck in the winter of 1916-17 and "went on for a whole week. It came out of the north-east. You couldn't see the barn from the house. We had to dig tunnels and run ropes from the house to the barn, and to the stacks to get feed for the stock. We were all at home and we had to stay there. We had lots of feed — '16 was a good crop — but we couldn't get the cattle out of the barn, and I don't know if you can believe this or not, but there was twenty feet of snow in the bluffs beside the yard. The trees were forty-five to fifty feet high, and they were filled right up. It was higher than the house, higher than the stacks.

"There was only one tragedy," Joshua went on. "There was a Ukrainian community east of here. The first night there was a wedding. You know how their weddings are, with celebrations going on for days. Most of them are lots of fun, but the host at this one had a bit too much to drink. He was a hot-tempered man, and at 4:00 AM he ordered everybody out of the house — into the storm. Nobody knew how bad it was at the time, and five of them never made it home. In the spring they found them, hanging over the fences, lying in the bush or on the fields.

"That haunted me for years."

5. Friends' Diaries

AT THE BEGINNING OF THE TWENTIETH CENTURY, all kinds of people kept diaries and letters. During my research, four sets of Friends' diaries and a number of letters were made available to me. The most complete set I got almost by accident when Laurie Crabbe decided to give them to me rather than throw them out, which he had been planning to do.

They were a set of yearly diaries, perhaps 2½ by 5½ inches each, and ½ inch thick, with a three-line entry for every day of the year. Fortunately, Laurie wrote small. One page is devoted to identifying the owner: height, weight, colouring; shirt size, including collar and sleeves; glove and shoe sizes; make of car and license number; insurance company. Populations of Canadian towns and cities are listed, along with festivals, holidays, and parcel post rates. First aid treatment for various conditions, including poisoning, are featured prominently. Weights and measures, distances, religions, safety rules, and how to calculate interest are all explained. One page is dedicated to the year's calendar, and two more to recording cash received and paid out. Virtually everything you might need to know for successful day-to-day living can be found in these little books, including how to treat turkeys with swollen heads (you use turpentine, though whether you rub it on the affected area or put it in their feed is anyone's guess).

The earliest diary was dated 1911. As the years progressed, so did Laurie Crabbe's artistic ability. Tiny pen-and-ink scenes begin to appear, remarkably life-like and vigorous. About 1960 he began to keep two diaries: the one strictly factual, the other much larger with anecdotes, observations, and ideas, with a beautifully coloured illustration of something that happened that day. Unfortunately, I did not have free access to that one. In the other, the notations were terse and written in the smallest script I had ever seen. Eventually I had to get a magnifying glass to save my eyes.

It was well worth it, for the entries are colourful as well as terse, and many tell a whole story in a few words: "Went to town to get new buggy. Had runaway. Came home in old buggy." And certainly a full, rich life was witnessed by the entry that listed the following: "Triplets to pure-bred ewe. Popes had 19 pigs. Franklin D. Roosevelt died today. Took 100 chicks in for Bessie. War stopped in Europe. Seeded barley this afternoon but we cut wood this morning." Dates of seeding, calving, breeding, and other farming events are duly recorded.

"You'd be surprised how many times you run to the diaries to check times and dates and things," Laurie told me.

His days were mostly filled with work. The only thing he ever minded about his life, he said, was the monotony. He didn't mind the cold. Heat and mosquitoes he could tolerate. Isolation was sometimes a blessing, and he enjoyed hard work. He would just have liked a little more variety. His diaries reflect this, although you don't see it at a glance. It's only when you realize that the corn patch he is hoeing is so large that it takes two men twelve days to finish it that the monotony of it sinks in.

Day after day the entries record ploughing, summer-fallowing, disking, mending fences, sharpening fence posts, cleaning barns, hauling loads of grain and hay and wood and rocks, building chicken coops, adding onto buildings, sending turkeys to Winnipeg, people dropping in, and himself going visiting and attending various meetings. He recorded the birth of the Dionne quintuplets the same way he recorded the foaling of his horses, the calving of his cows, the lambing of his ewes, and the number of eggs his hens had laid so far that season. On one election day he wrote: "Liberals won 49 seats Labour 5 seats Conservatives None. 30/100 inches of rain. Killed and dressed a sheep before breakfast."

Laurie Crabbe married Hannah Mary McCheane in 1918. The story was that Hannah Mary had "favoured" Laurie's older brother, David, and she was of a comparable age. But Hannah Mary had an older sister, Lydia, and Lydia wanted David, and she got him. Hannah Mary was left to turn her affections to David's younger brother, Laurie, which was convenient, in a way, for he was her father's hired man. Laurie, for his part, badly wanted a farm of his own, and what better way was there to get one than by marrying the farmer's daughter?

It was not uncommon for people of disparate ages to marry at that time and in that place. Marriage had more to do with who was available than with romantic notions of passion and love. Still, Laurie's marriage to Hannah Mary was not ideal: he was twenty-three and she was forty.

There were no natural children from the marriage, but they adopted a boy and a girl. The boy had severe digestive problems. They tried everything they could think of to bring him along. They prayed, of course, and brought the matter to the Friends for further help. Then one day Laurie was out canvassing for the poultry pool, and happened to pass a field where a Jersey cow was placidly grazing. Now, Jersey cows yield a very rich milk, hardly the thing for a baby with digestive problems. Nonetheless, Laurie had a sudden and powerful conviction that he should buy the animal. Accordingly, and rather to his own surprise, he approached the owner and made him an offer. The owner was surprised as well, but he sold the cow, and it was on her milk that the little boy finally thrived and grew. They never had another moment's trouble with him.

THE FRIENDS, LIKE ALL FARM PEOPLE, were helpful neighbours, so when Jack Saunders, who wasn't a Quaker, needed a hand in putting an addition on his house, Laurie Crabbe was glad to help. The project took several months, and Laurie frequently took his noon meal at the Saunders' table during that time.

It was at this time, too, that references to Margaret Saunders, Jack's wife, began to appear in the diaries. Laurie ran errands for her, drove her and her sister places when their husbands were busy, and took carloads of children — Margaret's, his own, and anyone else he could squeeze into the car — to fall fairs. Then, for a time, the references appeared in the singular: he took her on errands, or they went for a drive when they were both alone and the weather was pleasant. There was no sinful intent and no harm foreseen, but Margaret Saunders was a warm and appealing woman close to his own age, and Laurie was vulnerable with a wife much older than he, virtuous and loving though she was. Laurie was a robust forty-six, Hannah Mary sixty-three. Laurie fell in love.

It was an honest passion, and neither of them meant to hurt anyone. In due course, however, a child was born. He was the spitting image of Laurie, and the district knew beyond doubt that what the gossips had been chattering about for so long was in fact true. Not only that, but Laurie was incapable of disguising his pride in the child; it was obvious and startling to all who saw them together. When the boy was old enough, Laurie had him to his own home for weekends and holidays, and Hannah Mary cared for him.

The two couples made their peace with each other; no one knows how.

"Hannah Mary was very forgiving," according to one informant.

"She was meek and quiet and even-tempered," said another. "I never knew her to be angry."

"For sheer goodness, there was no one like her," said a third.

As for Laurie, he had been on his own since the age of twelve, with no close family ties and a less than ideal marriage. This was possibly the first time in his life he had either given or received genuine love, and it overwhelmed him.

Meanwhile, life went on, as it tends to do. One can only guess at the upheavals, the tears, and the recriminations that must have taken place among and between the two families, for none of this was mentioned directly in Laurie's diaries. But an indefinable air of bleakness had crept into the entries in the last months of one year, and the next year's diary had no notations at all except for a few rough sums regarding money he was owed. The diary for the following year picked up his life as if nothing had happened. But then references to the child began, and it is not hard to trace the bleakness back to the time when it all must have come out.

Jack Saunders was bitter, and perhaps heartbroken, and finally moved his family to Saskatoon, where the scandal died down. As for Laurie, he made the last years of Hannah Mary's life happy ones. He treated her with solicitude and consideration, kindness and affection. He built her a new house with central heating, running water, and electricity, but she only lived three years to enjoy it.

"After Hannah Mary died," Laurie confided, "my religion went right out the window. I haven't been to Meeting since. When she went, it shook me up so that if it hadn't been for the kids and the grandchildren, I'd have gone right to pieces."

Laurie lived as a bachelor for the next seventeen years. The Friends said he had a lot to grieve for, but he was not destined to live alone forever. Three years after Jack Saunders died, the one-time lovers' paths crossed again. This time Margaret and Laurie were able to marry. After a time they came back to Laurie's farm to pack up his things, for they planned to live in

A Community of Friends

British Columbia. Their presence reactivated old grievances, and feelings once again ran high in the district.

Then Daisie Lund, a long-time member of the Quaker community, had a conviction that she should throw a farewell party for Laurie and Margaret. The community was shocked to the core. So was Daisie, but Quakers don't argue about their convictions.

"It's the same as condoning what they did!" she was told.

"I don't care," she replied. "It's my conviction to have it and I'm having it."

She asked about sixty people, not knowing if any of them would show up. But in case they did, there was no place the party could be held except in the school house. This shocked the community even more.

"If it was in your own home," she was told, "it could be said to be a private party. But to have it in a public place would be another scandal!"

"I can't help that." Daisie was firm. "It has to be the school house. I haven't room in my own house for all the people I've invited."

She went so far as to plan a program centred around Laurie's life in the community, and lined up people to take part. As time went on, so did the talk, and several people backed out of the tasks they had agreed to take on. There was friction even among the Friends. One "had words" with another, and the other responded, "Thee sounds very self-righteous to me. If the two couples could forgive each other, then surely we ought to be able to."

Laurie Crabbe, hearing of the talk, phoned Daisie the night before the party and said that he and Margaret probably wouldn't be there. Daisie said all right, but she was having it anyway, so if they should change their minds they would know where to come. Her conviction was still very much with her, and she persevered, blindly trusting to the outcome.

The morning of the party, Laurie phoned and said that he and Margaret would come after all, but please, no program. Daisie agreed. No one had seemed prepared to take part in it, anyway.

Human nature being what it is, everyone who had been invited — and some who hadn't — showed up at the school house that evening. When Daisie and her husband Eric arrived, Laurie and Margaret Crabbe were in the middle of the room surrounded by old friends and neighbours. Laurie waved and called out, "It's all right, Daisie. You can go ahead with that program, I guess."

Things went off without a hitch. Everyone had a marvellous time, and when it was over, Margaret thanked Daisie from a heart overflowing with gratitude.

"If we hadn't had this get-together," she said, "I don't think I could have gone on with him."

"There was a lot of healing in the district that night," Daisie later told me, "and it was badly needed. If Laurie and Margaret hadn't felt forgiven by their old friends and neighbours, it would never have worked out for them."

As it was, Laurie couldn't believe how well he and Margaret got along. "We've had only one difference of opinion," he said, "and that was over the dog."

Laurie felt strongly that the dog should be allowed to sleep in the house. Margaret didn't.

The dog slept in the woodshed.

54

6. Convictions

Eric and Daisie Lund relied heavily on divine guidance in their lives, and "convictions" seemed to come to Daisie like blessings, although they frequently caused hardship and not a little bad feeling when other people didn't understand what she was about. She, too, often questioned them, but in the end her faith was unshakable.

Eric Lund's brother had died, leaving a wife and a little boy. The wife, Clara, remarried and had two girls. They were thought to be living a hand-to-mouth existence somewhere to the north, near Prince Albert. Daisie had begun to feel that the boy, Rusty, who was four years old at the time, needed a different kind of home. He had stayed with the Lunds from time to time since his father died, and knew his Uncle Eric and Aunt Daisie quite well. Daisie wrote to Clara, offering to take Rusty, but Clara replied quite sharply that she wasn't about to let go of her little boy, and that was that.

One day not long afterward, Daisie was working around the barn, thinking about nothing in particular, when these words came into her mind: Put down your fork at once and go into the house and write to Clara and ask for Rusty.

"I'll do no such thing," she replied. "I've done that once and been slapped down for it," and she went on forking hay. But the message was persistent and compelling. Finally, exasperated, she put down her fork and went into the house and did it.

The Lunds had invited another family for Christmas dinner that year, and it was a neighbourly thing to collect the Lunds'

55

mail for them before they came out from town. There was a letter from Clara. They could have the little boy, she said, if they came and got him, for she had no means of sending him. Neither had the Lunds. They had no money, literally. It was not an uncommon condition among farm families at the time.

Some time previously, Eric had arranged to exchange a stud colt for a load of timber with a man who lived near Prince Albert. The man arrived on Boxing Day with his son. He had felt a compulsion to come, he explained, and he was quite cross about it. It was extremely inconvenient. What's more, he didn't believe in things like that.

"But there it was," he said. "I had to come, and I had to come today."

While they concluded their business, the man's son went exploring around the barns and the outbuildings. He came across a filly that took his fancy, and he asked his father if he could have it. His father asked the Lunds if they would sell him the filly. He only had fifty dollars with him, but he hoped that would be sufficient.

Eric and Daisy had no reason to hesitate. They sold the filly, took the fifty dollars, and Eric travelled back to Prince Albert with the man and his son. He had no idea if the man was going anywhere near Clara's, but they reasoned they could risk it and fly blind. As it happened, Eric spotted Clara's place just before they reached the city. Eric got out and went to collect Rusty.

He found the boy asleep on a bare floor, wrapped in a leather coat. He was wearing a light shift, and had pulled on a lady's stocking for a bit of extra warmth. His neck was so thin he could hardly hold up his head, and there were open sores all over his body, the result of malnutrition and neglect. Eric committed a portion of his precious fifty dollars to buying underwear and socks and warm clothing, then he took Rusty to the bus station in Prince Albert. He asked him when he had last had anything to eat. Rusty replied that he didn't know — two or three days, maybe. All they could get in the bus station was a chocolate bar, but when they got to Saskatoon they went to a restaurant and Eric ordered substantial meals for them both. The boy wolfed his down. Then they visited friends while they waited for the next bus to Borden. Seeing the remains of a turkey dinner on the table, Rusty polished that off, too.

Arriving at Borden, they managed to hitch a ride to within a quarter mile of the farm. Eric carried Rusty the rest of the way on his shoulders, for the boy was too weak to walk. When Mary McCheane saw him, she said, "There's one you'll never raise." Daisie demurred. Why had God gone to all this trouble if he wasn't going to let Rusty survive? She washed the child and anointed his sores, and put him to bed in the bathtub, for that was the only place they had for him in their crowded house. She padded it well, and Rusty slept happily in it all winter.

When Daisie learned of the state of the home the child had come from — cold and bare, and everything in dreadful disorder — she wrote to Clara again, offering to take the two girls for the rest of the winter. She had no idea where she would put them, or how they would manage to feed two extra mouths in addition to Rusty's, but she felt she had to make the offer. It was refused. One of the little girls died a month later, and Daisie was grateful she had at least had the chance to make the offer.

"I'd have lived with the guilt a long time if I hadn't," she said.

For Daisie, there were no coincidences in this story — nor, indeed, in the story of Laurie and the Jersey cow, or of her farewell party for the Crabbes. They were each, she said, "just one more indication of the clear feeling I have that you're provided for, depending on the way you live."

7. MARY MCCHEANE

I WENT TO SEE MARY MCCHEANE today. The first surprise was the sign in front of her house:

Watch for Tame Badger Crossing Road

A year ago, apparently, Mary's son, Philip, found a baby badger wandering about, thin and crying, and brought it home. He and his mother raised it to adulthood, as they do with all strays. Its name is Digby, and it lives under their woodshed. It comes every night to the back door, where Mary feeds it leftover porridge, which it loves. It has tried to get back into the house, and has chewed a good eighteen inches out of the bottom of a thick sheet of plywood which was nailed over the door specifically to keep it out.

The second surprise was Mary McCheane herself. She's eighty-one years old, so it amazed me when this tall, white-haired lady, standing as straight as a young girl, came to the kitchen door. She ushered me into the parlour, where there was comfortable furniture and a pot-bellied stove radiating heat on a chilly April day. The dog accompanied us. He was an ordinary, middle-sized dog, of no fixed breed, and clearly middle-aged.

"What's his name?" I asked.

"Oh, we just call him Dog," said Mary McCheane. "He had a name, but we never use it. It's just Dog.

"Go and close the door," she said to the dog, who had settled himself by the stove. To my surprise, he got up, went to the door, and gave it a shove. It didn't catch, and Mary said, "You'll have to do better than that. Go and close it properly."

The animal went to the door, rose up on his hind legs, and gave the door a slam with his front paws. He came back then, giving Mary a look that clearly said, I hope you're satisfied. Mary broke off a bit of biscuit from a plate beside her and gave it to him. Dog was mollified.

When I expressed my admiration, Mary McCheane said, "Oh, he can do lots of things, can't you, Dog? Lie down."

It was what he had been intending to do all along, but he got another bit of biscuit for doing it when he was asked.

"Roll over."

He began to roll over, but ran into the base of the stove.

"You can't roll over that way," Mary told him. "You have to roll the other way. Come on now and do it properly."

Dog thought this over for a moment, made a couple of false starts, and then rolled over the other way and was rewarded with a piece of biscuit.

"Say your prayers."

The dog heaved a weary sigh, got to his feet, and put his head on his paws, his hind quarters comically aloft. I'd stopped counting the surprises by then, so it seemed almost normal when Mary summoned him to sit by her and laid a piece of biscuit on his nose. "On credit," she said, and went on talking to me. The dog never took his eyes off her; neither did he move. Not a muscle. Finally, she said to him, "Paid for," whereupon the dog tossed the biscuit in the air, caught it, and swallowed it.

Later, when I was getting ready to leave, Mary's son-in-law came in with a small, furry creature which turned out to be another dog. As soon as the dog spied Mary, he was up on his hind legs, prancing about.

"You've been teaching this one, too," I guessed.

Mary smiled and went to the fridge. She took out a piece of cooked meat and began breaking it into bits. "This one has to see his reward before he'll do anything," she explained, adding, to the dog: "You'll have to do more than that before I'll feed you. Roll over."

The little dog promptly dropped and rolled over, neat as a jelly-roll. Mary gave him a morsel, and he sat on his haunches and begged.

"Don't be silly," she admonished him. "You're just being lazy." She made a circular gesture with one hand. The little creature lay down and rolled over, and got his second piece of meat. Then he stood on his hind legs again and Mary scolded him: "That's not the way you're getting it today." At once, the little dog got down and rolled over.

"The first one is the hardest," Mary McCheane said. "Once they get the idea that you want them to do something, it's easy."

When I got into the car, there was a beautiful bunch of freshly cut pussy willows on the seat. I was sure Philip Mc-Cheane had put them there; it was the sort of thing he would do. Philip was a very shy man, Joshua had told me, and I wasn't to be surprised if I never met him, but every time I went to see Mary, there would be something to mark the fact that he had noticed. I thought it a nice, old-world kind of courtesy.

It was about 5:00 PM when I drove along the little back road to Wakes'. You hardly ever see another car on that stretch, and it was so quiet and beautiful that I stopped and rolled down the window just to enjoy it. There was a copse of poplar by the road, and the country smells of poplar catkins and fresh, cold air was wonderful.

Suddenly there was a tremendous roaring noise. I couldn't think where it was coming from, or what it was. Then from behind the poplars a great black cloud rose until it filled the bright sky and turned it dark. I closed the window, because the air was filled with dust and twigs, bits of paper and chips of wood. For five minutes the wind blew like a hurricane, and then it died as suddenly as it had come — an unexpected shock, an utterly impersonal fury.

No wonder the early settlers suffered breakdowns and panic attacks. In such a setting, so new to them, the elements must have seemed like enemies that had to be faced and overcome. Whispers of suicide, strange behaviour, perhaps even murder: these are all hinted at in the records they left us — hinted at, and then sharply turned aside. But the longer I stay here, the more I am impressed by the preternatural loneliness of the place. Experiencing these sudden changes of weather, continually getting lost (farmers speak of north and south while I think of left and right), it does not surprise me when I pick up hints of people who have grown as lonely and unpredictable, and sometimes as violent, as the elements.

Nowadays, of course, things are more accessible. There are good roads and more cars, and many more people. It can't be as frightening as it was in the first decades of the twentieth century. But even seeing it more or less civilized, I am still impressed by its isolation and the power of its presence. So, as I say, it does not surprise me to learn of the emotional price many people have paid in order to survive here. It has left its mark on them.

I met a woman who goes to the middle of her house when the wind blows, and stays there until it stops. I met another who shuddered when relating how, as a young bride, she had had to go alone to one of the Doukhobor villages to get a horse that her husband had arranged to buy, and found a street full of huge, hearty men, all talking in a foreign language and wearing strange clothing. She was terrified. But she got the horse, which tells you something about her courage and determination. Some of the Doukhobor women, those first years, actually pulled the ploughs themselves, having no horses, while their men worked for the railway to earn money.

Tomorrow morning I'll catch up with my notes. In the afternoon Nancy Penner is teaching me how to ride, or so she says. They have an old farm horse who doesn't much like to be ridden, but he'll put up with it. He's an honest horse, Nancy says, and won't throw me or try any monkey-shines. We shall see.

MARY McCHEANE WAS BORN Jemma Mary Saunders on January 18, 1891. She came to Canada when she was sixteen. Her father, Nathan, had arrived two years before, with four tons of settlers' effects. He bought cattle and horses in Saskatoon, only to have everything destroyed in a prairie fire the following summer.

"We had some bad blows like that," his daughter told me. "And we lost some animals to a disease called glanders. We'd bought some stock without knowing they had strangles, a throat disease. It's curable, but you have to quarantine them. If it was glanders, though, the government men came around and shot them. It was the only way to prevent the disease from spreading.

"The year I came, the only water we had was from the slough. We dug a hole beside it so the water could seep through. It kept the frogs out, but oh, I used to get thirsty. Kids used to drink the slough water, just dipping it up in their hands. I don't know why more of them didn't die of the typhoid."

What held young Mary Saunders in this country, despite the discomforts and the privations, was the animals and the riding. She'd been riding since the age of ten — side-saddle, in England. When she began to ride on the prairies, though, she was thrown badly, and her father traded in her English kit for a Western saddle, and he sent to England for jodhpurs so that she could ride astride.

A Community of Friends

"When I came here," she said, "heifers and steers had to be trained to be quiet cows and reliable oxen. Most settlers didn't have an idea in their heads how to go about it. The men would be away some place earning money, and the women wouldn't know how to manage the animals. Some of them put their cow on a chain because there was no place fenced to keep it, and the animals suffered dreadfully, what with the mosquitoes and the heat. I went around to the settlers' cabins and taught the women how to handle their livestock. We couldn't cure the mosquitoes, but I could say, 'Take your animals into a warm, dark barn, and give them a chance to get used to you. And don't ever stand where a cow can kick you, because if you do, she will.' Still, it was wonderful what the women put up with."

Mary lived with her brother and father in a two-bedroom shack. The bedroom wing was a lean-to, and the plumbing was outdoors. She hated not having tablecloths because there wasn't enough water to wash them. She hated enamel plates. She hated tin cups. She hated the mosquitoes. But she loved to ride. And they were never hungry, for her father provided well for them. And they were never cold. They had lots of good food and warm clothing.

Her mother had died when Mary was small, and she and a sister and two brothers had been brought up largely by an uncle. The uncle had bought one of the first radios in England with earphones. One day he was listening to it, and there was music playing. Suddenly he took the earphones off and flung them down.

"He felt threatened by his love of music," Mary explained. "He knew he could easily let it take over his life. But he was a Quaker, and he couldn't allow anything but God to take over his life."

She was quiet for a moment.

"I had a much more restricted feeling with my uncle than I ever had with my father. My uncle made me feel — well, I went to a chautauqua once, and all the time I had the feeling the devil was behind me with a pitch fork!" She laughed. "I wouldn't have the same fear now, going to a musical, but I wouldn't go unless there was some point to it. And I might feel uneasy, even yet."

Her father had taught her to read Friends' books, weighty tomes of historical biography and the like. Fiction was considered too worldly, and was denied them.

"But then, at Friends' school, they did a stupid thing. They let us read French novels. And how we learned French, we were so starved for stories! But we were all encouraged to draw and paint, and to keep journals. Any time one of us wanted to go to a lecture, we could. There were no restrictions on anything educational."

Like many Quakers, Mary McCheane had felt different from other people in England.

"Our clothes were different, always dark colours and plain styles, and we didn't go to ordinary schools like the neighbourhood children. They teased us because of these things, and the fact that our talk was plain — thee and thou. But when we came here, there was none of that. As far as clothing went, we had to take what was offered in the catalogues, like everybody else. In winter, I wore double-thickness riding breeches with Canadian wool socks — Arctic socks, we called them — and felt boots over them, just like the men. In summer, I wore divided skirts for riding. They were such a nuisance! It took yards and yards of material to make them — practically a whole skirt on each leg. The jeans that girls wear now are far more sensible."

All Mary McCheane's conversational paths eventually led back to her outdoor life, the riding, and the animals.

"One of the first summers I was here, I broke sixty horses," she said. "My father used to buy up carloads of wild horses from Alberta. They weren't standard breeds, but they weren't bad horses by any means. We got some very good ones that had been discarded by the Mounted Police — really classy horses, and could they travel! At home in England, if you ran a horse it wouldn't be long before it was panting and sweating, but the ones out here could really take it. Those were the kind of horses he'd buy. I'd break them and train them, and then we'd sell them at a profit.

"We hadn't enough fenced space, so in winter we just let the horses roam. They'd stay within about a ten-mile radius, and you'd get to know their watering places and where to find them. We'd go out every few days to count them and see they were getting enough to eat. No matter how cold it was, I always went out. I wore chaps in the winter. They were a protection when you had to go through rough places, and they were warm, too.

"When you're out to locate horses," she went on, "they get to know your smell, and they can tell when you're coming. If you're riding your own horse regularly, he gets to know what you're looking for, and he'll smell the other horses. When we found them there would usually be about twenty together on the lee side of a bluff, the big ones on the outside and the mares and colts in the middle."

Mary's father always kept a stud. At one time he had three, and he and Mary criss-crossed the country to all the mares. It was a good life, she said, being outside all the time, working with animals. It was good to have a father who allowed her to live a life that made her happy. It was good to be able to work alongside him.

Sharing the shack sometimes with Nathan Saunders and Mary and her brother Edward was one Jessie Green, a spinster with no family of her own. She helped out in the district when babies were born, or during haying or harvesting, any time a family needed a hired girl. When she wasn't working, she always found a home with Mary and Edward and Nathan. She was a bit odd, though. Going through three years of Mary's diaries, I found frequent references to Jessie Green. Most of them were some variation of the first, rather startling one: "Jessie Green had an hysterical fit today." The next most frequent reference to the luckless Jessie involved her varicose veins, which appear to have caused her considerable trouble.

For a long time, there was no mention of her at all. Then one winter day Mary was riding the range, and took a turn around an abandoned farm. Noticing that the well was unprotected, which was a violation of the law, she rode over to have a look. There, stuck halfway down, was the frozen corpse of Jessie. The diary at this point was spattered with the young Mary's tears, the ink blotted so badly in places that it was difficult to read. She recorded that her father had promised to come out with her as soon as possible to determine if it was Jessie for sure, and how to get her out.

The diary goes on for another week or so, and then another tearful entry: her father had that day accompanied her to the abandoned farm with its dangerously unprotected well. "It was Jessie all right," the diary reads, blotted with yet more tears. "She was the best saddle horse I ever had."

8. Two Families

When Betty Saunders married Neil Penner, two families decided to pool their resources. Betty was a niece of Joshua and Hannah Wake who, with no children of their own, could see a need for younger people to take over the farm in the future, and the Penners needed a place to start. Neil and Betty built a house a quarter of a mile from the Wakes', and added to it as their family expanded.

In the Wakes' house lived Hannah and Joshua, and Joshua's unmarried brothers, John and Billie. Joshua was the eldest, Billie the youngest. Betty's mother, Margaret Saunders, lived in the town of Borden. Another sister, Lydia, lived in England.

Billie travelled with Moral Rearmament — the Oxford Group, as it was originally called — giving talks and presentations throughout the country and the wider world. Founded by the evangelist Frank Buchman in the 1920s, the Oxford Group called for "moral and spiritual renewal" based on the "Four Absolutes: honesty, purity, unselfishness, and love." Later, as Moral Rearmament, or MRA, the movement became involved in political and social issues. Buchman held that moral compromise was destructive of human character and relationships, that moral strength was a prerequisite for building a just society, and that personal change could lead to social change.

When Billie Wake retired, he wanted to be called Bill, for it seemed to him more suitable for someone of his age and international experience. His relatives and neighbours dutifully called him Bill, but in their hearts he remained Billie.

Joshua and Hannah were quiet people, as was John, but they were not without spirit. I was there the first day Hannah used an electric washing machine. The wind died in the middle of the morning. The wind charger died with it, of course, and so did the machine, with the laundry half done. It was an interesting half hour while we transferred the lot to her old, hand-driven washer. Hannah, her face flushed with annoyance, talked the whole time. She expressed forceful views on electricity, winds that died, good intentions that back-fired, and on down the line until the miserable laundry was hung on the wretched clothes-line and the unspeakable machine put away for the week.

The Wakes were not large people but they were well-proportioned. All were slim, John in particular. He had cheek bones that stood out from hollow temples and deep-set eyes. He caught my interest from the start, he was such a quiet, serious-minded fellow. Occasionally he would contribute something to supper-time conversations, an observation or a quote that would start us all off on a different tack. Then suddenly you'd notice he was no longer there, and you hadn't seen him leave. It was John to whom the family turned when they were in need of straight thinking and good advice, and John who could go to the heart of a problem and see what the solution should be. He kept in the background, but his influence and moral authority were enormous. Billie especially depended on him.

When he was home, which wasn't often during the time we knew the Wakes, Billie was active and noisy. Unlike most of the family, Billie was deeply interested in music. He had records and tapes galore, and he played them loudly, leaving his bedroom door open so that everybody could enjoy the music, whether they wanted to or not. He would comment on this phrase or that, and draw attention to some aspect of it he was afraid you might miss, and he sang along whenever possible. If he wasn't singing he was humming, and if he wasn't humming

A Community of Friends

he was whistling. There was never any peace in the house when Billie was home.

The others never said anything, but they couldn't help being affected by their brother's constant noise and bustling about. When Billie had departed on another of his jaunts, the lines of strain disappeared from the family faces, and mealtimes were once again marked by light-hearted banter and easy silences.

After all four of them had retired to the town of Borden, I went to visit one day and there was no sign of Billie.

"Where's Billie?" I asked. "I thought he was home just now."

"Oh, he is."

They looked at me, sober and unsmiling. They stirred a little, shuffled their feet. There was a delicate clearing of throats. Then they looked at each other, and the corners of their mouths twitched. Hannah's melodious laugh erupted suddenly, Joshua chuckled, and John threw back his head and shook with laughter.

"Oh yes, Billie's home," said John, when he could speak. "He has his bedroom here, but he moved out to the coal bin."

"The coal bin?"

He gestured out the window. "Thou can see it from here."

One bedroom, apparently, had been too small to contain both Billie and his music, though whether this was from his point of view or his relatives', I never found out. So he insulated the coal bin, which was perhaps seven by ten feet, put down carpet and baseboard heaters, and lined it with shelves for his records and tapes. He had an orange crate with an electric kettle and a few mugs for coffee on it, and a couple of chairs. When he wasn't busy at the community centre showing his films and playing his music and giving talks, he spent his days and evenings happily in the coal bin, playing music and singing to his heart's content.

Once he undertook to entertain Nancy Penner and me with a half-hour of singing, both live and on tape. When we left,

Nancy said, "He seems to think he's a pretty good singer. What do you think?"

I tried to be tactful. If a man in his seventies could sing like that, I observed, how much better might he have been thirty years ago? Which was true. But Billie always had a high opinion of himself. He was aware of this fault, and from time to time tried to deal with it, but he never succeeded. It did lend him a certain charm. He was the best friend you could have when you needed one, and he was the most approachable of the Wakes, the most open and above-board. He was quite frank, for instance, about a streak of mental instability in the family. It was Billie who told me about his brothers Arthur and Henry, and his sister Lavinia, all of whom ended their days in mental institutions. When I found an article in *The Manchester Guardian* about the toxic levels of lead dust in some British towns the Wakes had lived in for several generations, and the mental confusion it could cause, it was to Billie that I took the article.

In my observation, what had been certifiable behaviour in those brought up in England had diminished to eccentricity by the next generation. In the current generation the tendency is toward a certain sensitivity under pressure, to which we are all heir from time to time. It seemed to me that the lead contamination could have been the root cause. They were three generations removed from it now, but some of the young people were still frightened by the "taint." It was the reason John never married, Billie said, and why he was afraid to loosen up and enjoy himself among people. I wanted Billie to have the Guardian article, because he was the only one who could bring it up with the rest of the family.

Joshua had a reputation for being "woolly-minded," but in the hundreds of conversations I had with him, he always showed a logical progression of thought about the history of the Friends, the faith, and the farm and community movements they were all interested in. Surely this was the product of intelligence and perception, I thought. He was full of enthusiasms, always alert for things of interest, for the unexpected, and he loved to be surprised. The day I arrived with a large-print Bible was memorable. He had been reading his battered old one with the aid of a magnifying glass. When he saw what I had brought him, he leapt from his chair and ran across the room, shouting, "Hannah, Hannah! Look what Betty's brought me!" He tripped on the edge of the rug, dropped the Bible, caught himself and retrieved the book in one swooping, magnificent gesture, and ended up on a stool, holding the Bible aloft, still shouting.

It was always rewarding to do things for Joshua.

THE FARM ITSELF WAS BEAUTIFUL. Not far behind the house was a small lake, surrounded by trees and shrubs. Beyond that was pasture, with stands of poplar and winding trails and gopher holes. The grain fields were mostly on the west side, along the road. The Wakes and Penners grew some wheat, and lots of brome grass and alfalfa.

Both families had strong opinions about the care of the land.

"You have to treat it with tenderness," Neil used to say. "You have to grow things that are natural to it, that's why we grow so many grasses. This land grows grasses naturally, left to itself, and we feel we should let it."

Joshua often remarked on the unnaturalness of summer-fallowing. "You never see a black field in nature," he would say. "A field, left to itself, is green. It wants to grow things. We believe that if it's not natural, it's not right. And I mean morally right, too. Nature knows what she's doing. God knows what's right for the land. The Penners and us, we've always tried to do what's right and natural for the land.

"Sure, we used to summer-fallow like everybody else. We used to plough deep, too, and for a long time we didn't think to question it. But we began to hear things from the agricultural colleges, and of course in the thirties we saw for ourselves how leaving the fields black left them open to erosion. You take Laurie Crabbe, now. He was a man who had to out-do everybody else. If he heard that a fellow had ploughed twenty-five acres in a morning, the first thing you know, Laurie would be saying casually that he'd ploughed thirty. But of course, he couldn't have ploughed very deep to get that much done. Well, that's Laurie's way, we thought. But when we found out what deep ploughing did to the land, we saw that he had been right all along, just ploughing up a few inches. We'd been ploughing deep because the theory was that when you turned up the deep earth, you saw that it was damp, and that was supposed to help the seeds germinate. But all it did was dry out the soil."

9. Valley Springs

ONE MORNING I WENT EARLY to the main house for my daily two buckets of water. John was there. "I'm going to Valley Springs this afternoon," I told him. "Ever since coming here, people have been telling me I ought to talk to Harry Hinde. I'm looking forward to it."

"Harry's very quiet and retiring these days," John said. "I doubt thou'll get him uncorked now."

From that point on, my chief aim in life was to uncork Harry Hinde. Another year passed before I had an opportunity. I did meet him that afternoon, however, and got one of the surprises of my life.

Joshua had said it was a perfectly straightforward road to the ranch, but there were a lot of novelties for someone who hadn't been over it before. On the level, the road was deserted. Not a soul did I see, never a car. But larks sprang up everywhere. There was a flock of bluebirds and a family of grouse, the mother in front and seven little fluff-balls running behind. On a distant ridge, three taffy-coloured horses stood poised, their tails and manes streaming in the wind against a blue, blue sky.

Where the road meandered off into a path, there was a right-hand turn and a Texas gate. Joshua didn't mention this, I thought as my little Mazda clanked and rattled across the metal rails. I could see why it was so effective in keeping cattle in; it nearly kept me out.

I drove. And drove. And drove. The far bank of the Saskatchewan River loomed ever closer, with no sign of the bank on this side. If there's a road down, I thought — which I was beginning to doubt — it must be precipitous.

It was. It snaked steeply to the right, then to the left, then to the right, one car wide with no turnoffs. I wondered what I would do if I met another car coming up, and if I'd be able to get back up myself. Halfway down, a large, level clearing opened out, sloping down to an immense pasture. I arrived just in time to open the gate for two riders coming up. It was Wes Ingram and his son Jimmie.

It was a half hour until I was due to meet with Wes's wife, Elsie, and it looked like a marvellous view from the edge of the pasture. "Is it safe to go in there?" I nodded toward the young bullocks milling around the slopes.

"Sure thing," said Wes. "They won't bother you none. Just keep close to the fence so's you can jump over quick if you need to."

The view was spectacular. The ancient river, a vast curve in both directions, glittered out of sight into the blue distance, much as it must have looked 10,000 years ago. It was easy to imagine herds of buffalo in the cloud shadows flowing along the far bank, to hear the wild and distant shouts of hunters in the wind that whistled endlessly across the dry grass.

Far below, on the river flats, a figure diminished by distance was tending a grass fire. He was walking along the dike tops, setting a torch to the grass here and there. The flames blew upriver. He followed and waited at the far edge. Suddenly the wind veered, as he must have known it would. He went along the far edge, setting more fires, which blew back on themselves until all were extinguished. I wondered why, and went along to see Elsie Ingram.

The Ingrams' house was close to the edge of the river bank. Another house tucked into the hillside near the road was occupied by Harry and Mary Hinde. Harry Hinde and Elsie Ingram were brother and sister.

A Community of Friends

The Ingram house had the usual outer room, this one full of boots and work coats, pails and garden tools. I went into the spacious kitchen and Elsie waved me to a chair by the window. She took the one opposite, sat down with a sigh, and looked out the window. All farm wives do that, I've found. When a truckload of young bullocks drove by, she sighed again and said, "I'm always relieved to see them go. I'm nervous having the men around them. Even so young, they're unpredictable."

The water supply caught my interest. Elsie explained that when her parents, Joseph and Martha Hinde (Uncle and Auntie), had come to Canada in 1912, Joseph had built the homestead on top of the hill. "For thirteen years we dug well after well, and got either bad water, a supply that didn't last, or nothing but blue clay." Often they had to haul water from the river, 400 feet below. When they realized that the plateau halfway down was full of springs, they moved the house down to it. That was in 1926.

"You moved the house down that narrow, twisting road?" I was incredulous. "How on earth did you do it?"

"The neighbours helped, of course. They got the house up onto blocks and a wagon bed. Then they hitched horses before and behind. The rear horses pulled up the hill, and the ones in front steered down. The ones behind kept the house from moving too fast. It was a chancy business, but they managed it."

Once established on the plateau, the problem was not how to get water, but how to dig post holes and such without getting water. There were springs at both houses and at the barns, and the source goes back under the pastures of at least two farms behind Valley Springs, including the Wakes'. One fall, Joshua and Billie were digging a silage pit for winter feed storage. Nine feet down, Billie lifted out a sizeable rock. Water gushed from under it so fast that by the time they had jumped out, it was up to their boot-tops.

When Elsie and Wes built their house in the early 1950s, they dug their well in the basement, for convenience. They had to work fast. "Men were down there with boards, holding everything back," said Elsie. "Wes lowered the concrete cribbing into it, and when the boards were pulled out, water rushed in from all sides. It filled the well almost at once. If you shine a flashlight into it, you can see the water flowing toward the river."

Outlets from the house's water system had to be put through the walls because of the high water table, and the septic tank floated when they first put it in. It had to be set high, and then covered with earth so it wouldn't freeze in winter.

The river itself was not so predictable. The house was two hundred feet above it, but one spring there was an ice jam and the river backed up behind it to within sixteen feet of Ingram's house. All the riverbank trees were under water, the irrigation system on the river flats was washed out, and when the jam finally broke and the water went down, all the river land for miles was covered with debris. "Chunks of ice the size of houses were scattered around," Elsie said. "Sticks and stones and trees and brush — oh, that was a clean-up job! A neighbour's straw stack was carried over three fences and ended up a hundred yards from our barn."

The river often rises high in the spring, Elsie told me. "One year it carried away a granary. Harry and Wes found the roof down by the power wires three miles away."

Wes came in, nodded affably to us both, and went to the sink. He sluiced water over his head and face, soaped and rinsed himself. Elsie got him a fresh towel, and he joined us, towelling his head vigorously.

"Remember that time we went to Langham, Wes?" Elsie said, picking up where she had left off. She turned to me. "We always took our cream to Langham, not Borden, and in winter we crossed the river ice. One trip we made, late in the season, we promised ourselves would be our last, and it nearly was.

"A trail across ice builds up into a ridge as snow falls and gets packed down. If the horses can stay on that, everything's fine, even when the ice is covered with water in spring. We got across all right, but we had to stay overnight. When we were coming back next day we came to a big, round hole, getting bigger by the minute."

"I got the horses going," said Wes, "and we went around the hole. But other holes started opening up, right in front of our eyes. We galloped as hard as we could, dodging the holes as they appeared in front of us. We didn't have time to think or be scared, we just went like the wind until we got across. That's when we were scared — afterwards! Half the town of Langham was out to see whether we'd make it."

"When I think of some of the chances we took!" said Elsie. "We were such greenhorns when we came to this country, ignorant of rivers — or at least rivers on this scale. And the light-hearted way we went skating. If there was ice, you skated. It never crossed your mind to wonder if it was safe. We nearly came a cropper on that river more than once, though often we weren't aware of it at the time."

Valley Springs was an isolated spot. Once the housework was done, there wasn't much for a woman to do except what is generally termed "men's work." Elsie did plenty of that, and enjoyed it, too. She and Wes were very companionable.

"Best thing ever happened to me was when I met her," said Wes. "Every spring we go for long walks, looking for the first crocuses, admiring the stock. We often ride out together. We've done haying together, roped horses and steers. It's all been fun."

A new dimension was added in 1962 when Elsie's brother Harry married Mary Needler. They were both in their early sixties at the time, and they set up housekeeping in the old homestead where Harry had always lived.

"It's been nice having a woman for companionship," Elsie said. "We have good times and good talks together, just like real sisters."

Wes thought the world of Elsie's parents, and laughed at the memory of Joseph Hinde — Uncle — listening to the radio and chuckling over the songs and soaps.

Elsie was a Quaker and went to Meeting when she could. Wes thought the Quakers were as good as any when it came to organized religion, but he didn't really believe in any church. His philosophy was neatly summed up in a couple of sentences: "There's one religious fellow that's always doing me dirt, and then apologizing for it. I wish he wouldn't do me dirt in the first place."

WHEN I WENT ACROSS THE YARD to visit Mary and Harry Hinde in the old homestead, it was with some apprehension and considerable interest. "You won't find them ordinary," I had been told. Since I had yet to find anyone "ordinary" in this community, the only surprise was that someone had said it out loud.

"Mary told me to tell you she's not going to tidy up for you," Elsie warned. This suited me fine, and I said so. I didn't want anyone doing anything different because I was going to be there.

"Yes, well," Elsie said, "this is a bit different."

Mary Hinde had a PhD in Classics and had taught at the university level most of her adult life. What she was doing married to a rancher after spending sixty years in a large city, and what she and Harry could possibly have in common, were things I meant to find out. And I was ready for anything.

The outer room was crammed to the roof with furniture which was obviously no longer in use but apparently too good to throw away. Nobody in his right mind would try to clear it out, I thought. You'd put a match to it first.

The kitchen seemed small, but only because it had so much furniture in it. Two magnificent old polished sideboards stood against two walls, with a table and chairs in front. Fridge, counters, and sink ran along the other two walls. Every available surface was stacked with books and papers, dishes, pots and pans. From the depths of the house a cheerful voice called out, "Hello! Come right along in."

I followed the voice and found myself boxed into a corner. *Where do I go from here?* I wondered. But there was a door in the corner, as I discovered when someone pushed it from the other side. It swung shut again. Another shove and, "In here!" called the voice. "Don't step on the cat!"

I grabbed the door, jumped over the cat, and found myself looking at the owner of the voice. Pure white hair swept back from a clear-skinned heart-shaped face, blue eyes full of warmth and friendliness. She was slender and youthful-looking for all her seventy-odd years, and wore jeans and a man's shirt, a baggy sweater over all. She did farm work and didn't mind getting her fingernails dirty. She was smiling her welcome, and I liked her at once.

The living room was as full as the kitchen, with every surface covered with books, magazines, and periodicals. Mary Hinde had a pleasant, gentle voice, and spoke at times with a deceptive vagueness. But whenever she wanted an article or a book, she knew exactly where to put her finger on it. I began to understand that the apparent disorder was, in its own way, highly ordered. Everything that was used regularly or referred to often was left where it could be got at easily. The treasured personal and family possessions of both Mary and Harry sat cheek-by-jowl with current reading material throughout the small rooms.

They each read widely, and held strong opinions on many topics. They shared religious and political beliefs, for Mary was also a Quaker. Indeed, they had met at Friends' House in Toronto, where they discovered that their interests were much the same. Mary had read everything Harry had read, and while Harry didn't know Latin or Greek, he had read everything he could get his hands on all his life. Neither of them had ever entertained thoughts of marriage, but when Harry had spent some time with Mary, he decided that she was for him.

"When I realized that Harry had intentions. . . ." Mary's voice trailed off, and she seemed to change the subject: "One day I was crossing Bloor Street, and this bus pulled up and stopped. As I stepped in front of it, it rolled forward ever so slightly. I put my hand out, which was foolish. I could never have stopped it. It was then I realized that Harry was like the bus. I had about as much chance of stopping him as I had of stopping that bus."

When we went to the kitchen for tea, Mary swept everything off the table with an efficient gesture or two, set a kettle to boil, brought out cheese and biscuits, and served it all beautifully amid the confusion. "I can't seem to function with closed cupboards and counters," she said. "But Harry thought I deserved better than his old-fashioned kitchen, and I hadn't the heart to discourage him."

I found it comfortable and relaxing, and as I came to know it better, I found it enchanting, the hand-made house among the cottonwood trees.

"I thought when I married Harry and came out here, I could make this place mine," she said. "I brought some heirlooms from my family, and I proceeded to arrange them, make some space, move things around and put some things out. For about six months, Harry watched me in silence. Then I discovered that with Harry, silence doesn't necessarily mean consent, so

I've left things pretty much as they were. I like long vistas, so I leave that door open for a good view through the window in the next room. And there's a pleasant view up the slope here. So you see" — smiling tranquilly — "we both have what we want."

There was a sound from the outer room. "That must be Harry," she said. "He's been down burning the meadows."

"Why do you burn the meadows?"

"Because they grow so thick they choke themselves out. We take off several hay crops a year, but we'd have no crop some years if it wasn't burned off frequently, it's so lush."

When Harry came in, I could scarcely conceal my surprise: cowboy boots, a western hat, leather belt, bearded face. I didn't notice if he was wearing chaps, and I doubt that he was actually carrying a brace of pistols, but it would not have surprised me if he had started yelling and shooting up the place. A friend of his later told me that, in his youth, Harry would have been quite capable of something of the sort — only without the shooting, for Harry, being a Quaker, was a pacifist.

He came in rather shyly to be introduced and to have his tea. As he came closer I could see that he had a gentle, kindly face, and strikingly candid, clear blue eyes. He spoke little, that first time, and only after lengthy and thoughtful silences. As I got to know him over the course of a year, however, I realized that my first impressions had not been far wrong, for he was a man of forceful spirit and powerful convictions, much given to swearing when provoked.

When Harry had gone back to work and we had cleared away the tea things, Mary announced that it was time to feed the chickens. She put on rubber boots and a straw hat, and we went across to Elsie's to get her vegetable peelings and leftovers. They talked comfortably, like sisters, Mary sitting on the edge of the table, swinging her leg like a schoolgirl. Then we took the pail of leftovers, added "shorts" to it (what's left over when

Betty Ward   81

wheat is milled and separated), and stirred it up with water until it was thick as porridge. Several cats were padding about looking interested, and Mary dipped out a spoonful. The cats snatched at long strips of turnip skins, moistly covered with wet grain.

"They know what they need," Mary observed.

We went to the ancient henhouse that stood in the lee of the hill, and Mary spooned big dollops of the feed in the shade outside, saying quietly, "Chuck, chuck, chuck." Hens ran up from all directions, big, prosperous-looking birds. They belonged to Elsie. The flock was two years old. It had originally been two flocks bought from different places at different times, and there was absolute bedlam for a couple of weeks as the hens fought out their pecking order.

"The head hen," Mary told me, "is a big, square-hipped, authoritarian bird. Even the rooster has to mind his manners around her."

We saw the rooster, strolling about in lordly fashion, but couldn't spot the matriarch. "We don't have a rooster every year," Mary said, "but Elsie kept one this year because she likes to hear him crowing. And of course, it's supposed to make the eggs more nutritious."

We went inside to gather the eggs.

"The henhouse used to be snugger," Mary said. "When Harry's father built it around 1927, it had double walls with bales of straw between. But over the years, the rats have made off with most of the straw and it's pretty cold in winter now. The hens don't seem to mind, and we have a heater in the drinking water to keep it from freezing. Even so, on a cold morning sometimes we have to put in a pail of hot water to thaw it out."

The nests consisted of a row of open boxes along one wall, and a row of closed ones on the other, with a third wall taken up with perches for roosting. We found one warm egg in an open nest, and that was all, so we went to the closed ones. Mary opened the box at the end. There was a hen in it, brooding darkly. Mary reached under it, but the hen would have none of it and pecked crossly at her arm.

"What's the matter?" Mary asked, quite as if the hen could understand. Apparently it could, for as she smoothed its feathers and spoke reassuringly, it settled down. Again she reached under it, and again received an indignant pecking.

"All right, all right," said Mary. "We'll leave you to your business."

A loudly clucking hen came sidling along a perch to an open nest, setting one foot ahead of the other with pigeon-toed deliberation. Clasping the perch firmly, three toes in front, one behind, she peered fastidiously into a box, clucking continuously. Another hen poked her head out to see who was making all the racket. The noisy hen chose her box and went in, making a few decisive comments as she settled down. The curious one withdrew.

The boxes all looked the same to me, but Mary said there were important differences to the hens. Sometimes three or four hens would be lined up waiting their turn in a particular box.

Back at Elsie's, I bought a dozen of the largest eggs I had ever seen. She said they weren't by any means her largest. "Commercial egg producers keep hens only long enough so they can also sell them for meat," she said. "They never get big enough to lay a really decent-sized egg."

Elsie's hens were kept outside in the sun and fresh air, to scratch on natural ground. Every afternoon they were fed the grain and vegetable mix, and the feeders in the henhouse were filled with wheat. Elsie believed chickens need to go to sleep with their crops full. Her method certainly works, though I was to see even larger eggs as I went around the district.

10. What's Right for the Land

Neil Penner is a thoughtful man with forceful ideas about farming. You have to do what's right for the land, he says.

"What you do has to be natural. Too many farmers look at the land in terms of dollars and cents. They'll look over a piece with a lot of trees and scrub, and they'll have this obsession to clear it, grow grain on it. That's cash. Fifty years ago this land was alive with animals, but they're nearly all gone now. The farmers never think of the deer and the smaller animals that find food and shelter in the treed areas. They cut down all that good wood and burn it in a big heap and it's gone. They drain the ponds where the ducks live and breed. But it's not natural for land to be without trees, without animals, without water. The thirties happened because farmers had cleared the land. All the topsoil was exposed to blow away. Everybody was at fault, but since we've realized here on our own farm that you should treat the land as naturally as possible, we've been growing grass on it, brome grass and alfalfa. It holds the snow in winter and prevents erosion in the summer. This whole farm is grass now except for the ponds and the stands of trees.

"So, we looked at all this grass and we thought we might raise cattle. We have no more than 150 at any one time, and we market the rest of the grass and it's profitable. I keep wondering what we can do to get across to other farmers not to clear all their land. You can't force them. They have to see for themselves that others are doing well and making a profit by treating the land gently. Since we've been doing it, I feel easier in my mind.

When you're doing right for the land you're doing right for yourself, too.

"Then there's the cattle. Sometimes I get fed up. They're a lot of work, and it's true that they're not natural any more, the way deer are natural. We've changed their breeds and their habits, even their instincts, and now they're coming into heat at all times of the year, and they often have difficult labours and need help giving birth. That's not natural. You've also got to know where they are all the time, so you can help them when they need it. We had a cow last winter that went off somewhere to have her calf, and for four or five days we searched everywhere. Finally we found her with the calf hanging half out of her, dead and frozen. Goodness knows how long the poor creature had been like that. We got the calf out, but the cow was so far gone we couldn't save her. It's times like that I don't think it's worth being a farmer. When I first went into cattle, things like that bothered me terribly. You never really get used to it."

I remarked that the bull didn't seem to know it was calving time, not mating season, and he said there were no bulls with the cows just now. They were off in the northwest pasture.

"But I saw one," I said.

He caught my meaning. "That'll have been a cow," he said. "When they come into heat they'll jump each other."

Nancy told of a cow that had calved in the middle of this past winter. They didn't know when she'd dropped her calf, but by the time they found her it had died of the cold. The cow had a swollen bag, of course, and was bawling horribly because she had no calf to relieve her, and she wouldn't let anyone near to milk her.

"We had a Charolais bull," Nancy said. "He was huge. He weighted 2,200 pounds, and his back was level with my shoulders" — Nancy's a good height, about five foot eight — "and he took to sucking the cow. He was so big he could get the whole bag in his mouth. He sucked her flat every time he got the chance."

"What did the cow think of it?

"Well, she never tried to butt him away. It must have been pretty uncomfortable, though. You can imagine how you'd feel, at forty below and a wet bag. Dirty old man."

TODAY IS ONE OF THOSE TYPICAL prairie days of relentless wind moaning in the chimney and rattling the windows. The sky is brown with dust. A cow is in my front yard, a common occurrence. I caught one looking in the window at me recently.

I've had lots of informal chats with the Penner children. Five of the seven are adults, so I can hardly call them children. Alan came over this morning. It was sunny and beautiful at the time. I sat on the step and Alan sprawled on the dry grass.

Alan and David think like their father about the land. Alan's point, too, was that natural land is never empty and black, as it is after summer-fallowing: "That leaves it open and defence-less to wind and rain. All over the country it's been eroded by wind and water. People say there's no way around it. But only about half of it's left, in these parts. The rest has blown away, or been washed away by rain and snow, because there's nothing to protect it."

He hates snowmobiles, except for people in the north who really need them. Anybody who hunts from a snowmobile might as well hunt from a plane. Neither way gives an animal a fair chance. Alan himself hunts on skis in the winter. That way, the animals have an equal chance. Hunting by snowmobile, though, "is just not decent. It spoils the winter peace, and animals have a hard enough time getting through the winter without being hunted by people on machines."

Alan only hunts in season, and only when there's a plentiful supply of what he's after. Of the prairie chicken who live on their farm, he says, "It's good for prairie chicken to be shot at once in a while. It keeps them alert and wary. And if you find a deer that's slow, or old, it's better to kill him with a clean shot in the fall than to leave him and know he'll spend the winter slowly starving to death."

11. Being a Quaker

NANCY WAS OVER FOR A WHILE, TOO. We got to talking of religion, and I asked her what it meant to be a Quaker for her personally. Her answer was simple: "It's to go to Meeting and sit for an hour and think about God and listen to him, and to think about how Jesus died on the cross for everybody. When Joshua talks out in Meeting, it helps. You need a focus to get you going."

Her parents have quiet times every morning for about an hour, and whenever her father feels things aren't going right, he sits down and has a guidance session, with his notebook handy to put down any thoughts that come to him.

"I've never actually had a guidance session," she confessed, "because I'd never know if the things that come into my mind are from God or myself. If it's something I don't want to do it's likely from God, I figure."

Here again is the punitive Old Testament God who seems only to want you to do what you don't want to do. I get the feeling from the young people that they have never been told what it means to be a Quaker. Their elders seem to have assumed that they would learn the faith through some kind of osmosis. When I asked Mary McCheane about it, she said, "We've muffed it somehow." But her daughter, Ruth Bergman, wonders how they could have taught them anything specific when they were so busy keeping themselves and their children housed and clothed and fed.

"Example is far more important," she said, "and we certainly got that."

The Penners have Bible reading every morning. Nancy said that, even if you're not paying attention, every once in awhile something gets through to you. The older Penner children were in favour of a Bible reading at the beginning of Meeting, to centre their thoughts. Neil thought it was a good idea, too, because even the adults fall asleep sometimes, just sitting there for a whole hour. But the Wakes didn't take to it.

Joshua once told me that when he was young they had Meetings at which the elders would read to the young people from George Fox and William Penn, and explain the doctrines and expound their meanings. Nancy hadn't known about that, but she wished they'd do it again.

"If we knew why we had to sit there for an hour, it would help," she said. "The reasons are always so vague."

She also told me that when they first got television, her father turned off the square dancing and musical shows because they were a wicked influence. He doesn't do that any more. Indeed, according to Nancy, "He just loves these programs."

When I questioned Neil about the dancing and musical programs, he said he had thought they ought not to be seen in his home by his children. They were too worldly. "But a life without sin is too bleak," he added.

It's difficult to imagine anyone faulting *The Sound of Music* as sinful. But Neil's religion is important to him. When we talked about the exodus of Quakers from the community — most of the Friends, when they marry outside the faith, go with their spouses — Neil said he thought the Friends themselves were to blame.

"We haven't made the faith real enough to our families," he said. "We talk one thing and we live another. If this wasn't true, how different things could be. Frank Buchman used to say, 'Give me ten men, wholly dedicated, and I will change the world.' If that's true," Neil said with real anguish, "there must be a terrible discrepancy between what we say we are and what we do."

From musicals we got onto other kinds of "sin," like games of chance. These are not allowed among Quakers, but chess is, and harmless card games like Snap. John Wake was fascinated with chess at one time, and he got very good at it. But he got so involved that he had to give it up because it was taking over his life.

"A thing like that takes a hold on you," he said, "and you're a slave to it."

He had a conviction that he ought to stay away from it, so he did.

"When man listens, God speaks," he said. "When man obeys, God acts. When a man does wrong, he's uncomfortable. When he does right, he's at peace. You don't have to know a lot of theology to understand that. Man has added on the theology and muddled the whole world."

JOSHUA ASTOUNDED ME ONE DAY by announcing that the Bible was not necessary, and that there were times he thought it would have been better if it hadn't been written at all.

"People can prove, or disprove, anything and everything by the Bible," he said, "and some of it is rank wickedness."

The Bible was interesting and could be helpful, but you don't live your life by what's written in a book; you live it by your own convictions, and those you get from God.

"When you've put God first, everything in the Bible falls into place and makes perfect sense. But you have to consult God first.

"Why, when William Penn came to this continent, he established a hundred-year peace with the Indians. He wrote to Friends back in England that the Indians had 'the inner light' and the same means of settling things — by what we call quiet times and they called a council. The Indians never had the Bible, nor did they know anything about Jesus, yet they had basically the same beliefs as the Friends. Anything that had to be decided, they decided by deliberation and thought, and everyone had to be in agreement before they came to a resolution. It's the same with the Friends. Quaker and Indian concepts of God were similar, both being rooted in a kind of mysticism. Indians didn't need the Bible to believe in the Great Spirit, and nor do we, really."

Joshua said that the Bible was written by holy people — not God himself, but holy men inspired by God. This means that human error can creep in. First of all, then, you have to deal directly with God. Every man and woman stands alone before God. The main thrust of George Fox's teaching and his revelation was that God was accessible to ordinary people. They didn't have to have a priest to intercede for them, they could approach God all by themselves. This was why there was so much persecution: the priests felt terribly threatened by the new religion because it would mean they weren't needed any more. Joshua said, "When you listen to God and deal directly with him in your own spirit, then everything in the Bible makes sense. It all falls into place. But without the Spirit of God, you can put all sorts of interpretations on the things you read in the Bible. The Bible is very useful and very plain to ordinary men. But first you have to listen to your inner light, to God speaking to you. Going to the Scriptures first is putting the cart before the horse."

EVERYBODY HAS A DIFFERENT DEFINITION OF SIN. One man told me it wasn't a thing you could define, because what was a sin for one person wasn't necessarily a sin for another. A man with a Quaker wife said he thought that anybody was good enough to be a Christian, but not many were good enough to be Quakers; he himself was such a sinner, in fact, that he couldn't even consider being a Christian.

One elderly Quaker gentleman said he and his wife went to an ordinary church when they moved from Borden. It had been fine, he said, until the minister started preaching that they were all miserable sinners.

"I put up with that for a couple of First Days [Sundays]," he said, "but he'd set me thinking, and I didn't like the direction he was going. So we stopped attending. The minister came to call, finally, to find out why we weren't coming to church any more, so I told him. I said, 'You're always telling us what miserable sinners we are, and I got tired of it. I may be a sinner, but I'm not a *miserable* sinner.'

"In fact," he went on thoughtfully, "I don't think I'm much of a sinner at all. I don't smoke, I don't drink, and I don't swear."

"Is that your definition of sin?" I asked.

"That about sums it up."

Neil Penner and I were talking of these things one morning as we sat in a patch of badger-brush waiting for a cow to deliver a calf. Neil said he thought sin was a separation from God, or separation from relatives or friends.

"If someone is bugging you," he said, "you have to tell them, even when it's their fault. Because it's still sin if it's separating you."

While we were deep in discussion, the cow suddenly got up.

"I'll bet she's had that calf!" I said, out of several weeks' experience of just missing the event.

Sure enough, she had. But it had been a breech birth; the calf was wrong end forward. The cow, busily eating the afterbirth, kept dropping it over the calf's head and face. The calf couldn't breathe, and showed no signs of wanting to. Every time Neil freed it, the cow dropped it again. The calf's muzzle was blue, and Neil said he thought it was too late to save it.

A Community of Friends

But it was still obviously alive, its eyelids were opening and closing slowly over big, soft brown eyes.

"We can't just let it die!" I exclaimed.

I moved closer. While I could not bring myself to try mouth-to-mouth resuscitation, I pummelled its sides and raised its head, trying to startle it into breathing. The cow stopped long enough to lean over her calf and bawl at me. I bawled right back.

"Don't be silly!" I shouted. "I'm a mother, too. I wouldn't hurt your calf!"

She seemed to understand, for she went back to her business and let me go about mine.

With an exclamation of disgust, Neil grabbed the calf by its hind legs and hauled it out from under its mother and dragged it away about ten feet, where he unceremoniously dropped it. The jar started the little beast breathing, but it had a lot of mucous in its nose. Neil thumped the calf to knock it loose so it could breathe more easily. The cow marched over, put her muzzle about an inch from Neil's face, and bawled loudly. Her message was so clear that we both laughed.

That evening, I saw the calf frisking about in the stiff-legged, stumping gait of the newly born, and though how it would have been dead had not we been there to rescue it. And that, I thought, was not natural.

12. Uncorking Harry Hinde

Harry Hinde finally "uncorked" a year after I'd first met him in his crowded house by the river. He and Mary came to Saskatoon every April for dental work, physical check-ups, and for Mary to do their income tax. They stayed in a hotel downtown, and Mary was glad to have me whisk Harry off for the three afternoons it took her to do the taxes.

Harry was born in 1902 in Birmingham, England, and came to Canada with his family in 1912. The first home the Hindes had was in Borden itself, beside the railway track. It was a main line, and there was a shunting train working there every day. The crew always stopped for dinner in Borden, and after dinner the engineer and the fireman would drive half a mile out of town and stop, claiming they had a hot box. What they were actually doing was going into the bush to shoot rabbits. They'd drive the train back into town with all the rabbits they could carry.

One day the station agent went with them, for he saw no reason why he shouldn't get in on a good thing. He came back on foot, madder than a wet hen. The engineer and the fireman had refused to back up the train for him, and he'd had to walk the half mile back to town loaded down with dead rabbits.

Joseph Hinde shot more than a hundred rabbits that year, they were so plentiful. It was the only meat the family had. Martha Hinde made rabbit skin coats for all the children.

Harry had gone to Friends' school in England, but when the family came to Canada he went to the local school at nearby Thistledale. The teacher boarded with his family, and urged his sisters, Elsie and Daisie, to continue their education. Harry would have liked to go on, too, "and nobody would have stopped me, but I felt I had to go out to work because we needed the money."

But all the time he was earning money, what Harry really wanted was to get into ranching. So did his father. It wasn't until Joseph Hinde and two of his sons were able to get a quarter section each that they realized their dream. They borrowed some money from a relative in England and put it all into fencing.

"We fenced most of our land and quite a lot of unoccupied land," said Harry. "There must have been nearly two and a half sections we fenced, and that was more than we had cattle enough to justify. So we took in cattle for other farmers from all around, and that brought in a little cash.

"In a way, that was the start of the Community Pasture," he said. "We'd had the idea for it, but it wasn't until a man named Schroeder died that we were able to expand. Schroeder had just taken a lease on 10,000 acres and put up eight miles of fencing when he died of the flu. His whole farm was sold off, and his wife sold the rights to half the leased land, the fenced part, to Arnold Larsen. Orchards and Elliotts got the other half. Larsen fenced the remaining, and Orchards and Elliotts put in another ten miles of fencing. But these were farmers. They didn't have one good saddle horse among the three of them, and they really didn't have any idea how to run a ranch. Elliotts were United Empire Loyalists from Ontario, and Orchards had been farming in Manitoba — a very different kettle of fish from here.

"A bunch of crooks built a snug little den in the rough banks near the river. They made home brew and transported it in a democrat. As a cover-up, they sold beef from cows they'd rustled. In the end they got caught because they were selling their meat too cheap. Some butchers in Maymont, fifty miles away, complained to the police that somebody was underselling beef in their territory, and it was unfair competition. The police sent a man who camped on the river bank for a week, waiting and watching. He never built a fire or did anything to give himself away.

"He got the evidence he needed, and the police made a raid and rounded up eight or ten of them. They'd had stills hidden in the bushes, and they got water from a spring. They'd even cut a narrow strip through the bush so they could send signals across the river. They'd rigged up a phone, and they had a boat on the bank below, and they took the hooch out that way. Part of what gave them away, of course, was that Larsen and Elliott were twenty-five head of cattle short that year. They didn't have anyone actually looking after their cattle, so the crooks had rustled to their hearts' content. They had a good thing going for them for a while, all profit.

"The reason this sticks in my mind is that, after that — in 1918 that was — Arnold Larsen came to me and asked me to look after his pasture. That was the real beginning of the pasture. I was sixteen at the time. I ran the pasture for Larsen for a year. I had a hundred cattle, and Larsen had a hundred. Anything over that two hundred, from other farmers wanting their cattle looked after, we'd split the fee. We weren't short any cattle that year.

"I'd spend two days at a time riding the pasture and the fences, and seeing the water holes were full. There was one place with thick brush which I figured just had to have water. If you crawled through the brush, you could hear the water trickling somewhere underneath. We chopped out a whole lot of brush and found it. We got a flume and ran the water to a trough below, where the cattle were. I've seen 600 head of mixed stock drinking from that trough, and the water level never went down more than six inches. By the time the next lot of cattle and horses came down, it'd be full again and running over. It just welled up out of the ground. It looked like running sand. Before we were through, we had 1,500 head of cattle in that pasture and I was riding four days a week, looking after it.

"I'd found out how to run that many cattle and that big an operation by writing to old George Valentine. He was a well-established rancher and took a tremendous interest in what we wanted to do. He ran the Matador, the first community pasture in Saskatchewan.

"The Matador Company was from the United States, and they'd been running it for about thirty years. They got a great kick out of sending 4,500 steers up to Canada every year, in bond, so after they'd fattened up at Matador for two years, they could send them to Chicago and flood the market. It wasn't supposed to be done, sending cattle back and forth across the border, but they had a private arrangement with the Canadian government.

"Anything that died had to be photographed and accounted for. There were several bad winters when they lost hundreds, all piled up in the coulees. There was one pasture they called the Bone Pile. There were five acres of bones gathered there. Some people came to skin them for hides. In fact, some US cattlemen got their start skinning Matador cattle.

"George Valentine wrote me a five-page letter, telling of all the different ways we could run cattle. He suggested I come down and spend some time at Matador and see it for myself, firsthand, so I did. I stayed three months, through spring, summer, and fall, and I'm sure glad I did.

"Matador is south and west of here. It's twenty-five miles across and pretty near square. It was divided up into townships, and the round-up pasture was a section and a half — that's 960 acres — and the only small pasture they had. There was a set of corrals for the horses, near the bunkhouse. The horses would forage overnight, and when it was my turn to be horse-wrangler, I had to get up at half past two to run them into the corrals. The cook rattled his triangle at 4:00 AM. Days like that, you'd think you'd been up and working for half a day already and it was only 9:00 AM.

"We had seven horses to ride — each of us, alternately — and we'd change horses two or three times a day, depending on how hard we were working them. It's wonderful country, mostly hills and no bush. I wasn't there for fall round-up, but I was there for the summer one when we shipped 4,000 steers to Winnipeg.

"One time, toward the end of roundup, about ten of us were cutting out some steers from a herd. Old Valentine, he was getting old but he could ride like a fool. This day, from over the hills we saw a cloud of dust coming. It was old Valentine, larruping this big steer along. The steer was covered with foam, and when he got close enough Jesse Perrin, the foreman, said to me, 'You take that steer up to the coral.'

"I was riding a kind of nervous horse called Redwing, and I started off with the steer. We hadn't gone more'n two or three hundred yards when the steer turned and faced me. He wasn't going to go any farther. I yelled and galloped at him, and off he went. But then he did it again. Old Valentine had sure been licking him along! So I galloped at him again, but instead of turning like before, he came at me. He lifted up my horse and threw him over backward. The horse scrambled to his feet with the steer horning him from behind, and stood there pawing. As I was trying to turn him, the steer came at him again, and Redwing turned tail and ran toward the corral. I ended up with the steer chasing me into the corral and all the way around it. When I got to the gate I slammed it in his face. I thought he'd come right on through, but the gate held.

"Turned out he was an outlaw steer. He'd got away every round-up, and had been living down in the brakes for two or three extra years. He must have been five or six years old, and he had a set of horns like this!" Harry gestured with his hands. "At supper, none of the guys would believe what had happened, so I dared them to go into that corral. They pooh-poohed me and went outside. One guy got into the corral, and the steer took after him. I never saw a guy go up a fence so fast. He was just a foot ahead of the horns. Another guy went to the opposite side and waved his hat inside the bars. The steer came at him as if he meant to tear the corral apart altogether. Finally Jesse Perrin came out and put a stop to the monkey shines before we wrecked the corral.

"They kept that steer for three or four days without food or water. I felt badly about that, but we really didn't have anyone to spare to look after him, and nobody felt very sympathetic. When we did get around to him, we knew what we had to deal with, so there were ten or twelve of us on horseback on either side of the gate when it was opened. We whooped him out and headed him along, directing him to a bunch of steers waiting to be shipped out. He was caught for good and all, that time, he couldn't get away.

"But you know, that steer had acted just like a Mexican fighting bull. I'd done a lot of travelling with stampedes and rodeos, so I'd managed to keep my own seat on the horse, clinging with my legs, and the forty-pound saddle helped. When he lifted my horse, I guess my feet were high enough that I wouldn't be touched or rolled on. But the horse was sitting right down with his legs stretched out in front of him.

"The only time I ever saw a real, wild stampede was just before round-up. There were 1,500 head of cattle, and five of us driving them. They were all young heifers and steers — what we call dry stuff. We were just getting them through the round-up gate into open country, and for no reason we could see, those cattle just burst out of there. They sounded like thunder. I and a fellow called Nels Hagen, we had to ride as hard as ever we could, trying to get them to run in a long circle. They must have run pretty near a mile before we got them, so they were running into their own back end. A township's big, we could have lost them.

"I used to ride in the rodeos, saddle broncs and steers. I stuck on most of them. Sometimes I was thrown, not often, and I made good money at it. I don't think Mother approved of me riding in the stampedes, and sometimes members of Meeting used to talk to Father about it, but none of them ever said anything to me. We never did anything against our own consciences, and Father never said he thought I shouldn't do it.

"I came back from the Matador because I was needed on the farm. Otherwise I'd have stayed. The pay was good and I liked the life."

On the second afternoon Harry Hinde announced, after a lengthy silence, that he had broken thirty-eight bones. "After I fell off the barn roof last winter and broke my leg, Dr. Paulson said that he guessed I'd broken pretty well every bone in my body by now. I told him I hadn't broken my neck yet, and he told me to save that for last."

It got to the point, when he was young, that every time word came that Harry had been hurt again, his mother would go into hysterics, for "most of the bones I broke," he said, "I broke right at home in the pasture.

"We used to have a horse we called the Bronc, because he sure could buck. One day I went to mount him, but just as I got my foot in the stirrup he moved back. Ordinarily I'd have taken my foot out and started over, but I'd just had that boot fixed, and the shoemaker had left a nail sticking out of the sole. I couldn't take my foot out because the nail had gone straight through the leather and into the wood of the stirrup. The Bronc started

A Community of Friends

to go around and around, not knowing what was wrong, then he panicked and I swung back against his heels, still caught by my boot. He gave me a fair kicking, I can tell you! He didn't actually step into my mouth, but he stepped on my face and knocked all my top teeth out. He broke my breast bone, some ribs — eleven bones altogether, that time."

Another time, Harry and his sister Elsie were taking some horses to the pasture. Elsie turned back at sunset, but Harry expected to be away two or three days. He was riding the Bronc again, and for no reason the horse suddenly fell flat on its side.

"Of course he unseated me," Harry said, "but he got right up again, and before I could do anything he was galloping cross country as fast as he could tear. We figured out later that my spur had got tangled with the lariat on the saddle horn, but all I knew at the time was that he was dragging me against his heels, kicking me at every step. He knocked me out, of course, and eventually he yanked my boot off. When I came to I couldn't move a muscle, couldn't raise my hand, couldn't do anything. At the same time I realized that I wasn't expected home for three days."

But Elsie, going over the last hill toward home, happened to look back. She thought she saw a galloping horse with a saddle but no rider. She couldn't be sure, but she didn't want to take any chances. She came back and found her brother where the horse had left him. He could talk, but he couldn't move. They had to send for an ambulance. He was taken to hospital in Saskatoon. They found no broken bones, and he was released after only four days. Ten years later, after another accident, X-rays revealed that the bones of his shoulder and arm were a mass of cracks, like a river with tributaries, and they all came from the time the Bronc had dragged him.

"Why on earth did you keep a horse like that?" I asked.

"He was a good horse except for those two times," Harry said.

There was another horse, a mare, who was easily spooked. A prairie chicken once flew up in front of her and she started to buck. Eight years before, Harry had hung onto a bucking horse and eventually ridden it back to the corral — where he had to be lifted off, for the violent movement had yanked his pelvic bones apart. Eight years later, on the mare, he could feel the bones ripping apart each time she bucked, and he knew he had to dismount somehow. So he threw himself off and landed on a pile of rocks.

I winced. "Does it get any worse?" I asked.

"Yes, it does," said Harry mildly. "Falling on the rocks knocked me out. My head was covered with blood and, like before, I couldn't move."

Also like before, someone saw a horse with a saddle but no rider, and eventually found Harry. Once again he was taken to hospital in Saskatoon. The pelvic bone was fractured in three places and ripped six and a half inches apart. They couldn't put him in a cast because they couldn't get the bones together, and the reason they couldn't get the bones together was that Harry hadn't bothered going to a doctor the first time and over the years the bones had adjusted to being apart and now would not fit together the way nature had designed them.

"They were giving me dope every three hours," said Harry. "They were scared I'd become addicted, but before the end of the three hours it hurt so bad I wouldn't know what to do. Sometimes I'd beg them to give me more.

"For about a month and a half they kept me in a kind of frame, about an inch above the bed, with webbing that went underneath and around me. When they lowered me onto the bed they packed thirteen pillows around me and move me to a new position every three hours, day and night. I'd be comfortable for maybe twenty minutes, and then the pain would start again."

A Community of Friends

He lapsed into silence, but with Harry you learned to interpret the small signs and gestures that meant he wasn't finished.

"With pain like that," he said eventually, "there's no room for thinking, or praying. You just endure."

I suggested to him that perhaps it was his faith, nonetheless, that had made it possible for him to endure, for there were times the doctors did not expect him to survive. He moved in his chair as if he were reliving the pain, and there was another long silence. Then he said, "Later on, faith helped. Not at the beginning, but later on when the pain eased a bit and I was able to think. When I first got out of bed I couldn't use my legs at all. I had to learn to walk all over again.

"The family got rid of the mare. They got rid of the Bronc, too, and I didn't care if I never got on a horse again."

"But you did."

"Oh yes, I rode again. I had to look after the pasture."

MARY ARRIVED at about five o'clock for supper. It was touching to see how glad Harry was to see her. He helped her out of her coat, gave her a hug and a kiss. They'd only been apart a few hours, but the afternoon had been hard on him. Talking was becoming increasingly difficult. Mary thought it was because of all the falls he'd taken, being dragged and kicked by horses. In any case, when Mary was present, Harry was happy to leave most of the talking to her.

There was one more thing I wanted him to give his mind to that day, however. I had been asking everyone for their definition of what it meant to be a Quaker, and now it was Harry's turn. He gave the matter his usually thoughtful attention, then announced that it was simply doing the will of God.

"How do you find out what the will of God is?" I asked.

"It makes more sense if you put it backwards," said Harry. "I feel happiest when I'm doing the will of God, doing what I know is right. When I'm doing what's right, everything seems to fit. It's like being in a state of grace: you know when you're in it. You can feel it. But you don't stay in it; it needs working at. A lot of times, Meeting helps you stay in it."

Mary said that a state of grace was what you felt in a "covered" Meeting, when the Spirit is present and everybody feels it. "Everybody feels covered by the Spirit, surrounded with it. It's a wonderfully rich and joyous feeling, a kind of singing gladness inside. It makes you feel blessed, as if you could stay good forever.

"Those Meetings are quite rare," she went on, "although they might happen oftener than we know, because the experience is such a profound one. If nobody says anything, friends are apt not to know that it was happening to everyone. We're told, as well, that if we come to Meeting with hearts and minds prepared — that's to say, taking thought before coming, not chatting or gossiping — a covered Meeting is more apt to happen."

"I've heard a rule of thumb for speaking out in Meeting," I put in. "If you feel like speaking, don't. If you feel like speaking a second time, don't. If you feel like speaking a third time, consider it, because it might be from God."

"Speaking out at Meeting is like dropping a stone into a pond," Mary said. "You should wait until all the ripples have died down before you disturb it again. It's called 'centring down.' You never speak in reaction to what someone else has said. On the other hand, you shouldn't hold back if there is something you really feel you ought to say."

I asked her how she had come to join the Society of Friends, for I knew she hadn't been born to the faith. I asked her if it had been an intellectual decision, or perhaps a conversion.

"It can be anything from a blinding flash to a slow realization, or a conscious decision," she replied. "When you want to join the Friends, they don't give you a particular book to read or a set of rules, although the Borden group has a short set of written rules you must agree to. The request to join is submitted in writing, then the Meeting sends two elders to speak with you about your faith and your outlook. They take the results back to a closed Meeting and decide whether or not to admit you to the responsibilities of membership. Because friends care for one another in various ways, and there is no minister, it falls to every member to care for every other. When someone is in trouble, the Friends cast around to find the one who would be most helpful. It makes you feel very cared about and supported, but at the same time you have to be very caring and supportive yourself."

I asked Mary if she had found many differences between the group at Borden and the Toronto Meeting she had come from. She said there weren't a great many. The written rules was one, but she didn't object to that. What she did object to was the decision regarding liquor and smoking. "At Yearly Meeting we've thrashed this out with warmth, if not heat," she said. "Some wanted outright prohibition. Others felt that prohibition was not only improper, but that it missed the point. I felt it did. Moderation in all things — or most things. As Aristotle said, with some things you have to 'hit the mean extremely well.' You wouldn't want to be 'moderately healthy,' for example."

We discussed whether Friends' communities were still viable, or if they were becoming just another church. Mary felt strongly about it. "A Quaker minister, or elder," she said, "is in a different relationship to his congregation than the ordinary. Other churches developed out of Christ, through Peter, from Catholicism down to Calvinism, Lutheranism, and other Protestant groups, but ministers in the Friends have been released to do service to their Meeting. Some Meetings have paid ministers; Toronto Meeting was originally a paid ministry, but when one family withdrew its support the Meeting went back to being unprogrammed.

"There are people of maturity and grace in any Meeting, and they are chosen almost by unspoken agreement. Gradually the Meeting comes to a realization that they are speaking consistently out of wisdom and spiritual intuition from God, and they are recognized. And there are also ministers who go about speaking to other meetings, ministering to other communities. People like this, who are especially gifted, ought not to be paid for it. It mars their gift, and it makes it very difficult for them to remain untouched by their position."

Many Friends hold the same opinion, but others argue that the labourer is worthy of his hire, and that everybody has to make a living. Mary shared Joshua's view that, if people feel called to ministry by God, they need only trust that God will see to their livelihood, too.

HARRY COULDN'T REMEMBER ANYTHING he would classify as a hardship. "When everybody's in the same boat," he observed, "you don't have any standards for comparison, so you don't notice whether things are hardships or not."

He remembered how he and his brothers and sisters learned to throw rope, practising every evening after supper. It was a skill they all needed, yet they didn't regard it as a chore. "It got to be almost an obsession with us," he said. "We'd practise and practise, the way some people play games."

Another thing he regarded as a kind of game was the gathering of rocks during noon hour. "It took the horses longer to eat than it did us," he said, "so we'd amuse ourselves for half an hour or so, gathering rocks and piling them up in handy places for hauling to the railroad in winter. We were farthest from the river, and nobody thought we'd even consider hauling rocks, but in the end, we hauled more than anybody."

Rocks are still being hauled to that river, tons of them, to fill in the big bend by the railway grade. The river keeps washing them downstream, and the rocks have to keep coming to protect the railway.

While Harry didn't remember hardships, he did remember the things he enjoyed, such as the electricity, when they got it. "We never had a wind-charger," he said, "but we had a little outfit that ran on a set of batteries. You'd run it for four or five hours, and that would charge the batteries, and that much would last two or three days. We'd run it in the evenings — that was one of our chores, getting it going. When it shut down, the batteries carried on and we had lights from that. We had a vacuum cleaner, too.

"Having the electricity changed our whole egg production," he went on. "The hens used to quit laying in winter, but when a light is on it fools them and they keep on laying. It isn't the cold that stops them, it's the lack of light."

"Were you ever lonely?" I asked.

"Oh, no!" said Harry. "With our big family and all the 'neighbouring around' we did, not to mention all the chores that had to be done, there was no time to feel lonely. If there was a spell of real cold weather, you'd ease up on all but the necessary chores, and stay in the house, but there was always reading you wanted to catch up on."

I asked him about wood, always a concern on the unforested prairie when you had to rely on it not only for heating throughout the winter but for such things as harness trees and fence posts. Being on the riverbank, I had assumed Harry's family would have had no trouble securing a reliable source of wood. As it turned out, there was lots of poplar, but they had to go north for good, hard birch.

"The birch was fifteen miles to the north," Harry said. "Every year we'd make an expedition to get it. It was in a pretty inaccessible spot, about two hundred feet down on the right bank. We'd get the birch, and haul it all up to the top, and cart it home. We kept ourselves in birch about a year ahead, all the time, because it takes a year for it to cure. We'd strip the bark off — it rots fast if you don't — and saw it into the right lengths and put it in a cool place to cure. We kept a supply of poplar all the time, too, and we used it for just everything: fence posts, railings, pens. The original barn was all built of straight poplar poles.

"We had some logs of spruce that we got out of the river," he went on. "We had to scrounge anything and everything we could from wherever we could, and it used to be fun to see how resourceful we could be, how we could get something out of nothing. We'd go out when the river was in flood — that would be in April, maybe even late March, after the ice went out, and then again in June when the melt came down from the high mountains. We had a twelve-foot boat that we'd paddle to get logs. We'd go down the creek connecting our slough to the river, and out toward the middle, paddling upstream. You'd see all kinds of stuff coming down — whole trees with their branches still on, ice floes with sometimes a dead deer on it or bits of buildings. You'd grab hold of a log and bury a hook in it, and hook that into a loop of wire attached to the boat. Sometimes we'd get two or three if we were lucky, but one was more usual. We'd be so busy trying to keep it following, that when we'd look up to notice where we were, we'd think the banks were rushing by, and it was us, rushing downstream! It was amazing how much we got out of that river.

"One time we were out in the evening and there was all kinds of stuff coming down. The river was high that year, and we could hardly believe our eyes: a whole island, a hundred yards long, with trees fifteen to twenty feet high growing on it, the whole thing just floating down the river. We figured it must have been a sand-bar where a lot of wood and junk piled up — you could see it, about eight feet deep — and trees had grown up in it, and when the high water came the whole thing floated loose. It was the most amazing sight."

"Wasn't it dangerous?" I asked. "Did you ever get swamped?"

"I suppose it was dangerous, but we never thought of it that way. For us it was an adventure, and if we'd needed an excuse for doing something dangerous, well, we needed the wood, that was all. We never got swamped."

When Harry was about fifteen, he took a short course in mechanics in Saskatoon. He learned how to take machinery apart and put it back together. He also learned how to put a hot-water system into a farm, then went home and did it.

"Professor Evan Hardy taught that class," Harry said, "My, he was a wonderful teacher. He could take that big class — and there were fellows in it over forty years old — and hold their attention for two hours at a time. He could tell you a formula for doing something that you could then go home and do yourself. I made a sketch of a water system in a scribbler, showing distances and lengths. It took me a year to put it all together. We didn't have money for extras like a water system, but Professor Hardy had me all fired up and I was determined to have one.

"I went to Saskatoon and found a storage place where Uncle Joe Wake kept some old hand fittings. Most of them were scaled-up pretty bad, and not strong enough to take the city water pressure. I picked out a few that were usable once I got them welded up. The few new parts I had to buy cost me fifteen dollars. That was the only expense of the whole thing."

"How did it work?" I asked. I didn't believe for a moment that I'd be able to understand it if he did tell me — plumbing has never been one of my hobbies — but Professor Hardy had caught my interest, too.

"We had one big tank alongside the cook stove in the kitchen," he explained, "with a pump for pumping water upstairs. The tank upstairs was above the bathroom, and it was twice the size of the one in the kitchen. You'd pump the tank upstairs full of cold water from the downstairs tank, then fill up the downstairs tank again and the stove would heat that water. There were two pipes between the upstairs and downstairs tanks, one for hot water and one for cold. When you turned on the tap upstairs, the hot water came up from the kitchen tank. The cold water in the upstairs tank went down at the same time as the hot water went up. Being heavier because of being twice the size, the cold water's weight would push the hot water up. We had a drain for the basin and bath, but it wasn't big enough for a toilet. We would have needed a four-and-a-half inch pipe for that, so the toilet was a chemical one.

"That drain was another accomplishment," Harry said. "It ran into a sump hole outside. It was twelve feet deep and four feet square. Bob and I dug it. My, it was a nasty job cleaning it out, but it lasted ten or twelve years before we had to. We had a sink in the kitchen too, and a pump for soft water from a cistern in the cellar, which is more than we have now.

"You know, I got more satisfaction out of putting that water system in, for nothing but my own ingenuity and hard work and a pittance of money, than if I'd been able to go down the street and buy everything from a store and pay somebody else to do it."

Harry was silent for a moment. He rearranged himself in his chair, then surprised me by saying, "I guess you thought I'd forgotten that you wanted to know my definition of sin."

As it happened, I had.

"Well?" I asked.

"Breaking the Ten Commandments," he said.

One morning when I went over to get water from Wakes', Hannah and Joshua and John were sitting around the dining-room table having a cup of coffee before getting at the day. They'd just finished their morning quiet time, and invited me to sit down and have a cup with them. I was glad to. Any opportunity for stories is welcome.

The first crop of wheat Joshua planted was lost to a flock of geese. He was about twenty years old, and he had a hundred acres sown to wheat. He'd cleared the land himself, got out all the roots and stones, raked it and ploughed it and planted it. It was ready to harvest when he went out to look at it one morning, and was surprised to see the whole field moving. As he got closer, he could hear the honking and gossiping that geese do among themselves, and when he realized what was going on, he was horrified. All his work gobbled up by a flock of geese!

He tried to scare them away, running and shouting, but they just looked at him, he said, mildly surprised, and moved aside a bit as he came among them, and moved back again when he ran someplace else.

"They weren't the least afraid of me," he said. "Probably knew I had convictions about killing them — or not killing them."

They ate virtually the whole crop. There wasn't enough left for it to be worthwhile trying to harvest. I asked him if he'd ever had an experience like that again, and he said he never had. But the geese had reminded him of the eagles. I'd read about the eagles in Edward McCheane's diaries, but Joshua told the story in greater detail, and of course his point of view was quite different from that of the youthful Edward.

The Friends do not all share Joshua's convictions about guns. Edward had one, and he shot prairie chickens and rabbits for food. One day he shot a golden eagle. He was rather pleased with it at first, as a trophy, but when he discovered it had been a mother with two chicks, he felt terrible. He brought the little things home, and everybody took an interest in them. They roosted on the handles of the shovels and rakes that stood outside the back door of McCheanes' house. When they wanted food, which was often, they squawked dreadfully.

McCheanes had a dog named Bruce, who loved to hunt gophers, and every gopher he caught was delivered to the eagles. He kept them well-supplied, and everyone was surprised at how well they did, and how quickly they grew. One hot Sunday in July, everybody was at McCheane's for Meeting when someone, looking idly out the window, saw the eagles making off with the family cat. They rushed to the rescue.

"I don't think they could have got far with it," Joshua said, "but it certainly gave us a turn."

As the birds gained in strength and size, they widened their field and began hunting on their own. A visiting Friend, a woman, had heard about the great birds and expressed an interest in seeing them. So Joshua hitched up an open buggy and away they went. He drove to a place where the eagles were often seen, and sure enough, there they were, taking off from a rise in the land, as is their habit. Joshua called to them. Hearing a familiar voice, they wheeled and came in low over the buggy. The lady instinctively put up her arm to ward them off, and one of the eagles just as instinctively landed on it. Its talons went right through her wrist.

"But she was made of pretty good stuff," Joshua remembered. "I told her to sit perfectly still and I would pry its talons off her, toe by toe. She sat as still as a statue, never said a word through the whole thing."

13. WHEN IN DOUBT

THIS IS THE LARGEST PART of Quaker belief, the cornerstone: when in doubt, consult God.

"At one time nobody believed you could have direct communication with God," Joshua told me, "and then George Fox found out you could. He had been searching for spiritual peace for years. He had gone from church to church, seeking out the best minds he could find, but none of them could help him. Then one day he was sitting alone on a hillside, overcome with hopelessness. He wasn't thinking of anything in particular, but suddenly he became aware of a voice inside his head, talking to him. And it said, 'There is one, even Christ Jesus, who can speak to thy condition.'

"When George Fox realized the implications of this simple statement, he was electrified. He was off and running to tell anyone who would listen to him that Christ's teachings were available to anybody, at any time; that people could have first-hand knowledge of God; that it applied to your whole life, not just Sundays; and that special buildings and ministers were not necessary. So the early Quakers gathered for worship without any program or arrangement, nor did they have appointed ministers.

"The early Friends believed that out of an energetic and expectant silence, God might use any one of them as a minister. When they first experienced this, they were so moved that they shook and trembled; they quaked. That's why people began to call them — us — Quakers.

"When George Fox began preaching that you didn't need clergy or churches, the established clergy felt threatened. The early Quakers were persecuted, jailed, hunted down, abused, even killed. George Fox went to a Sunday service in Swarthmore once, and when the minister said something Fox disagreed with, he got up and said so, and explained why. The deacons of the church escorted him briskly from the premises and threw him over a stone wall into the cemetery."

Joshua was very particular that the history and beliefs of the Fritchley Meeting at Borden be set forth accurately. There was a general unity of belief among the Quakers from 1648 until about 1800, he said, but by 1840 "false doctrines" were beginning to create trouble. There were many small things that contributed to the eventual split in the faith, but the major cause can be found in the works and preaching of two men, Joseph John Gurney and Elias Hicks. Gurney, a prolific writer and preacher, advanced the view that the Bible was the only guide for Christian life and conduct, thereby denying the basic Quaker conviction that God was the primary guide. Hicks took the opposite view, questioning the authority of the Bible and even denying the divinity of Christ.

The group at Borden had never deviated from the teachings set forth by George Fox in 1648. As far as they knew, Joshua said, they were the only ones who still adhered to these basic principles.

Nevertheless, most Quakers I asked could not define their faith with any clarity, and nearly all of them said they had had no specific training in what it meant to be a Quaker. Only a handful of the older ones seemed clear on who and what they were, and they said that even if the faith died out in their community, it wouldn't matter. They were serenely certain that God was on the job, and that the faith would pop up somewhere else, under a different name and clothed in different words. They had

A Community of Friends

seen it themselves when the Moral Rearmament movement came to the district in the 1930s.

ALL THEIR LIVES THE FRIENDS had gone to First Day Meeting, and many went to Fourth Day Meeting as well. But for many of them, their hearts were no longer in it. There didn't seem to be any life in the group any more. Their lack of form had become a kind of form in itself, a sort of rote, devoid of meaning for many of them.

Then in the thirties had come a representative of the Moral Rearmament movement. From the Friends' point of view, MRA's basic principles were sufficiently similar to their own that they could embrace them wholeheartedly. MRA was not, in itself, a religion. You could belong to any church and still be part of the movement. Many of the Friends found Moral Rearmament rejuvenating to their own faith, and all were interested, if not entirely in accord with it.

MRA taught that if you applied four basic principles to whatever you wanted to do, and saw that it was honest, pure, unselfish, and loving, then you had to be doing the right thing. Another thing they held in common with the Friends was the custom of coming together for silent guidance. MRA called it their "quiet time," only it differed from the Quaker practice in that they wrote down the thoughts that came to them and shared them with the group afterward. This process had been regarded by some as a kind of confessional, only without the constraint of confidentiality imposed upon a Catholic priest or a consulting psychologist. Some dreadful scandals came to light, a few marriages broke up, and several businesses were destroyed before the MRA people realized that the process had to be governed by discretion.

There were other abuses, as well. One wealthy widow became known as a soft touch, and many people went to her saying it had been their guidance that she buy them a new suit or shoes, or some other useful item — and the good woman always did. By and large, however, the group was well-intentioned, especially when their founder, Frank Buchman, was alive to keep them focussed. Moral Rearmament did many people a lot of good. Once Buchman died, however, the focus began to shift. They decided things were far too easy, and they had better have something that was defined as a "sin," a discipline for them. So they decided that sex was a sin, except for procreation.

The Friends discussed this uneasily. Some of them tried to live that way, with disastrous results. Eric Lund, Harry Hinde's brother-in-law, was not himself a Quaker, but he had great admiration for his wife's faith, and believed that MRA started to go off the tracks at that point.

"They thought they had to have something that was a sin," he said, "and sex was the first thing they thought of. How logical was that? You learn to live with and enjoy the good things of life. You wouldn't make yourself sick by eating like a hog; it's the same thing with sex. You have to build a philosophy within yourself that you can live by and be comfortable with, and know your own right from wrong. I don't think Christ was the kind of person who was rigid about these things.

"With MRA, sex is wrong. With Quakers, liquor is wrong. I think each of us is entitled to our own belief about right and wrong. Isn't that what the Quakers teach? That everyone stands alone before God and is answerable only to God? We're all good enough to follow what Christ taught, but we're not all good enough to belong to a religion. There are some things that not everybody is able to do.

"Personally, I wouldn't join any religion. Of course it's easier to follow a pattern of rules and regulations than to decide your own. But then you lean on them. You don't think out your own ethics and moral principles. If you're following a set of rules laid down by somebody else and the elder says, 'Pray now,' you do it instead of praying out of your own conviction. When you're on your own, a very simple philosophy can keep you knowing right from wrong."

Harry Hinde said he knew when he was doing right because of the way he felt when he was doing it, and Eric Lund approved of this theology.

"I don't think the Lord is concerned with people doing wrong," he said, "so much as he is with their willingness to do right."

14. A NOVEL EXERCISE

It was a dull, cloudy day, quite cool, and I went to see Mrs. Smith. She used to clerk in the Borden grocery store, and knew just about everybody in the district. Her husband, who ran the store, is now dead. Mrs. Smith welcomed me warmly into her house. She introduced me to two other people whom she had brought home for lunch. One was a tiny, fragile-looking old lady with enormous dark-brown eyes and an extraordinary wig of the same colour which was far too big for her head. The other person was a young minister who served the district. I judged the man to be in his mid-thirties, rather phlegmatic, solemn, serious-minded, unmarried, and devoted to his flock. He smiled readily enough, though he was really without much humour. He brought the fragile lady into town every week for medical treatments, and she thought he was wonderful. So did Mrs. Smith. They both sang his praises so openly and fulsomely that in his shoes I'd have been dreadfully embarrassed, but he just sat there and let it wash over him.

According to the two women, he was a "wonderful musician, just wonderful!" Indeed, there appeared to be little he could not do, including playing the violin with two bows so that it sounded *exactly* like bagpipes. This struck me as a novel, though singularly useless, exercise, but the ladies thought it a marvel, and oh! how they wished I could hear him, he was really quite remarkable. Was it possible? They turned to him in entreaty. Might he . . . would he. . . ?

Well, he just happened to have put his violin in the trunk of his car as he was leaving, and yes, he could be prevailed upon to get it and entertain us with a tune or two.

When he had departed for his fiddle, the little fragile lady was all a'flutter with adoration and expectancy. Mrs. Smith was likewise full of praise, but she kept within the bounds of reason. The young man reappeared with his violin and, hardly saying a word, took it out, tuned it, fitted it under his chin, took the two bows in his hand and began to saw away, one bow above and the other below the strings. He played half a dozen Scottish tunes, and they did indeed sound much as if they had been played on bagpipes. He played as he seemed: stolid, faithful, and without colour, but in tune.

What do you say to a man after such a performance? We thanked him. In the ensuing silence, I said that it was really quite remarkable — it *was* that — and that it really did sound like bagpipes.

The ladies looked at me. I was clearly expected to say something more, so, always dutiful, I said brightly, "It's enough to make you want to dance the Highland Fling."

The succeeding quarter of an hour was one of those nightmares that come back to haunt you. The ladies pounced. Could I dance the Highland Fling?

"Heavens, no!" I said. "I haven't danced a Highland Fling since I was twelve years old. There is no way I could do it now."

I would have done better to have uttered a simple no. As it was, they clamoured and insisted. If I had done it as a child, they reasoned, I could do it now. Oh, come on. You can remember. It would be such a pleasure. Think of it! The minister playing his violin and me dancing the Highland Fling! What a *treat* it would be! I kept on saying "No, I can't, I really can't," and they kept on saying, "Yes, yes, of course you can, you're just being modest," and, "Come on now, just for us," and so on and so on. Then I made my last mistake. I said, "Even if I could, I'd knock over all your furniture, prancing about like that."

Never again will I make qualifying statements about anything. They moved the furniture back against the walls with a speed and vigour I wouldn't have believed them capable of at their age. Then they sat there, looking at me expectantly. The minister was standing at the ready, bows poised, beginning to sound out a few chords and tunes.

Dear God, I thought. *What am I going to do?*

God, or someone who sounded very like God, replied rather sternly that I was going to get up and do a version of the Highland Fling that had never been seen before.

And, please God, will never be seen again, my conscience added.

And I suffered. *How* I suffered! When I figured I had stumbled about sufficiently to satisfy the most demanding tyrant, I stopped and sat down to expressions of admiration and delight, and a round of thoroughly undeserved applause.

If, as a journalist, I had ever trapped or tricked people into telling me things they didn't want to tell me, or manipulated conversations to that end, I atoned in full measure on that day. Never have I been more embarrassed and mortified. Never have I felt such an idiot. Once the little lady and her enormous brown wig had departed with the minister, however, Mrs. Smith gave me an excellent interview. So I came out of it bloody but unbowed.

15. In the End, We Return to the Beginning

IT WOULD BE A STRANGE SUNDAY INDEED if there were no guests drifting in for visits and tea at the Wakes' house. I was in the kitchen setting out cups and saucers one Sunday afternoon when Hannah escorted a mutual friend into the next room to take off her coat. I heard the friend say, "By the way, Hannah, how is Henry? Is he still living?"

"Oh yes," said Hannah. "He's eighty-two now, and a perfect patient, the doctors say."

"Has anyone been to see him recently?"

"Joshua and John went over a while ago and he was the same as usual, and he recognized them. He's always so gentle and appreciative when people go to see him, Joshua says. Never a moment's trouble for the staff, always does as he's told. You would think...."

"Yes, I know," the friend said, sympathetically. "You'd think if he could act so normal in an institution, he ought to be able to be that way at home, too. When was it he was committed?"

Hannah said she couldn't remember, but he had been quite a young man. "It was long before my time here," she said. "Joshua said when he first went that way — Henry, that is — Mrs. Wake threw her apron over her face and burst into tears. She said, 'Oh dear God in heaven! Not Henry, too! Not Henry!'"

Hannah's voice broke. I could hear her blowing her nose as she and the friend moved to the kitchen.

"And of course," she went on when she had recovered, "with Arthur, and then Lavinia, and finally Henry, I suppose the poor woman wondered where it would all end."

Belief in "the instability" was so strong in the family that every one of them was fearful of it. This became more clear as I thought back on it. Joshua, in relating the story of how he and his father came to Canada, had never mentioned that Arthur had been with them, too. And in reference to Lavinia's early death, Joshua had said merely that no one really knew what she died of — which was true, as far as it went. It was only when other people spoke casually of Arthur or Lavinia, assuming that I knew about them (as everybody else did), that I began to piece the story together. When I learned that they had died in the mental hospital at North Battleford, many things became clear.

Hannah had been quite frank once she realized I knew about the instability in the family, but she told me only what I asked. She never elaborated. So while I knew she had found Joshua's mother difficult, I had had no idea that Hannah had almost left because of it.

The elder Mrs. Wake had been an extremely hard person to live with. It was believed that her marriage to Hugh was a loveless one. Hugh was charming but impractical, it was said, and Margaret, his wife, came from a poor family, socially well below Hugh's. Joshua could not get along with her "for beans," according to one informant, and while Billie was fond of saying what pals he and his mother had been, they had in fact quarrelled constantly. When Billie wanted to go on the road with MRA, she had told him, "Guidance or no guidance, you're staying here and getting on with the work." One wonders how much of the family's trouble was due to innate instability and how much was a response to the stresses of more powerful personalities.

Had their faith been a help to them? With Joshua and Billie, it was clear that it had been. But for John, who, I was told, had once been a merry fellow who laughed a lot and enjoyed a good time, it seemed to have been a tremendous burden. When I knew him, he still had a lively sense of humour, and often I saw him doubled over with laughter. But his face in repose wore a look of constant anxiety and suffering. His faith must have sustained him through the ever-present fear of instability, I deduced, but at the same time he seemed overwhelmed by the duties and responsibilities of living a good life.

He spent most of his energies striving for perfection. "It says in the Bible," he once told me, "'Be ye therefore perfect, even as I am perfect.' Jesus wouldn't have said that if it wasn't possible for us to be perfect."

John, it seemed to me, had skated very close to the edge. Once he had realized that the instability could affect him, too, it had gripped him with a paralysing fear and blighted his entire life. And of course it was a real and justifiable fear. He had seen what happened to two of his brothers and one sister. It could happen to him, too.

But with John, the fear seemed to have been woven into every fibre of his being in a way that it had not with Joshua and Billie. It cropped up in ways that seemed to have nothing to do with anything: a dread of too many people around him, or too much noise. He had strange symptoms, of which he said once, diffidently, "Some day I'll tell thee about my trouble — it's physical."

If ever I saw a man riddled with non-physical dread and constant fear, it was John. It was a measure of his fear that he always referred to his trouble as a physical one. He and Joshua were about the same size, but John always seemed smaller, and I think this was because his spirit had been diminished by fear. He had an air about him which suggested that he felt gauche and awkward, as though people were able to perceive his siblings' mental instability by looking at him.

On the other hand, he had a reputation within the family for clear thinking, and they all looked to him when problems arose. I once took a knotty problem to Billie, and Billie went immediately to John. John would not have talked to me about it, but with Billie as intermediary, he had insights and solutions which I valued and put to use. A lot of John's wisdom came to me second-hand, but it was no less valuable because of that.

John lived well into his eighties, always on edge, never really happy, never feeling really well. It seemed unfair that he had to work so hard at being good, or perfect, and have so few rewards for it. He felt he had no choice but to be solitary, yet he suffered dreadfully from loneliness.

Billie was out in the world the most, and was consequently the most worldly in his outlook. Still, a good deal of his travelling money was contributed by his brothers, chiefly John. It would have been unthinkable for John to have gone into the world in such a fashion, and he felt that helping to pay the expenses of a brother who could was his duty and his pleasure.

Billie Wake was a prolific writer. He wrote the story of his life in its entirety, including an account of his conversion when he encountered the Moral Rearmament movement, his subsequent fall from grace, and how he found his way again. He wrote maxims, poems, and stories to illustrate moral points, and even a play or two. He was a wonderful friend and an admirable, if somewhat self-centred, man.

But in the end, we must return to the beginning. My introduction to the Quakers at Borden, the love that grew up between us, the hospitality and generosity they unfailingly showed to my husband and to me: all are synonymous in my mind with the life and example of Joshua Wake. For Norman and me, there was nobody so endearing.

Alas, you cannot get the flavour of Joshua by reading about him in these pages. I cannot give you the warmth of his presence, or show you his excitable enthusiasm as he explains points of faith. You cannot see him, as I did, running his gnarled but still flexible fingers through his shock of sandy hair. You cannot see the bushy eyebrows, raised almost to his hairline and sticking out a bristling inch from his brow, nor the deeply-set blue eyes; nor hear his voice, still with a tinge of Birmingham, rising in excitement, his partial upper plate falling — clack! — and unconsciously tucked back into place as the inspired words flow on. He is mature and he is wise, he is childlike and woolly minded. He has always been like that: easily dejected but just as easily subject to great enthusiasms; gently saddened by the sorrows of his friends and himself, but quick to find the road back to grace; full of colour and quicksilver, full of humanity and compassion and innocence, always believing the best of everybody.

"Except that ye be as little children, ye shall in no wise enter into the kingdom of heaven," declares the King James version of the Bible. Joshua's most conspicuous characteristic was this same child-like faith and trust in God. Three days before he died, Joshua, with a look of pure rapture on his face, turned to Hannah and whispered, "I wish I could tell the whole world how wonderful it is!"

"He was halfway into heaven right then," Hannah said.

And heaven will never be the same, now that Joshua is there.

Betty Davis was born in Stratford, Ontario in the 1920s and raised in the relatively newly formed United Church of Canada. Working in Toronto as a journalist while she studied music, she met Norman Ward, then doing a PhD at the University of Toronto. They came West in 1945, where Norman was to take up a one-year appointment at the University of Saskatchewan, and never left. They had six children; Betty gave concerts with the symphony and finished her music degree; and eventually she took up journalism again with the Saskatoon *StarPhoenix*. Betty is now in her 80s; *A Community of Friends* is her first book

A Community of Friends is set in Adobe Caslon, a typeface designed by the American typographer Carol Twombly in 1989. Twombly based her designs closely on the work of William Caslon (1692–1766), the first great English typecutter. Caslon was a near-contemporary of George Fox, founder of the Religious Society of Friends (he was born the year after Fox died); it is likely that this is not the first time their names have been linked.

Titles and chapter heads are set in Trajan, also designed by Carol Twombly, and released in 1988. It is based on the inscription at the base of Trajan's Column in Rome.

Edited, designed, and typeset by Donald Ward, who also designed the cover.

Illustrations by Brigid Ward.

The cover is a composite of two photographs, one taken by Norman Ward and the other by Betty Ward, on the bluffs above the South Saskatchewan River, circa 1951.